When **Sally** Met **Agile**
Experience Agile through a captivating story

Manav Agarwal

Copyright © 2024 Manav Agarwal

All rights reserved.

ISBN:**9798340898180**

Preface

When I set out to write "When Sally Met Agile," my goal was simple: to make learning about Agile methodologies feel less like studying a textbook and more like following an engaging, relatable story. Too often, guides to Agile can feel abstract, rigid, and disconnected from our day-to-day experiences. I wanted to change that. I wanted to create something that resonates with people on a personal level—something that makes you nod your head in recognition, perhaps chuckle at the similarities to your own experiences, and leave you feeling inspired and empowered to embrace Agile principles in your own work.

The idea behind this book is to bring storytelling to the world of Agile in a way that feels authentic and practical. Whether you're new to Agile or just looking for a fresh perspective, Sally's journey will guide you through core concepts and help you see how Agile thinking can fit into your own workflow. The power of storytelling lies in its ability to make even the most complex ideas digestible and relatable. By following Sally's ups and downs, I hope you'll find yourself immersed in the story while learning valuable lessons along the way.

You'll notice that each chapter ends with a section called "Manav's Thoughts." This is where I step back from the story to share more advanced insights, discuss key Agile concepts in greater depth, and recommend resources for further exploration. If you're looking to build a foundational understanding of Agile, feel free to focus primarily on the story. But if you want a more holistic view—one that not only introduces you to the basics but also encourages you to dive deeper into Agile methodologies—then I highly recommend you spend some time in the "Manav's Thoughts" sections.

However you choose to read this book, whether you immerse yourself fully in both the story and the thoughts sections, or you focus just on the basics, I'm confident you'll come away with a strong understanding of Agile principles and how they can transform your approach to work.

This book is for anyone who has ever felt overwhelmed by rigid processes, for those searching for a more flexible and responsive way to manage projects, and for those curious about how to foster a culture of continuous improvement—whether in their professional life or beyond.

I'm truly excited to share this journey with you, and I hope that as you follow Sally's path, you'll find inspiration, practical knowledge, and maybe even a few laughs along the way. Thank you for picking up this book. I believe it will not only help you understand Agile but also inspire you to approach your work with a fresh, adaptive mindset.

Happy reading, and welcome to the world of Agile!

Warm regards,

Manav

Contents

The Struggles of Frameworks — 6
   When One Size Fits None — 6
   Manav's Thoughts: — 12
Embracing Agile Values — 14
   Learning to Love Change (Without Therapy) — 14
   Manav's Thoughts: — 18
Mapping Dependencies — 20
   Untangling the Corporate Spaghetti — 20
   Manav's Thoughts: — 26
Cross-Team Collaboration — 27
   Herding Cats Across Department Lines — 27
   Manav's Thoughts: — 33
Introducing Custom Sprints — 34
   Racing at Your Own Pace — 34
   Manav's Thoughts: — 39
Customer-Focused Innovation — 41
   Mind Reading for Beginners — 41
   Manav's Thoughts: — 47
Scaling the Sally Model — 49
   Growing Pains and Sticky Note Shortages — 49
   Manav's Thoughts: — 57
Adapting the Sally Model — 59
   When Your Framework Needs a Facelift — 59
   Manav's Thoughts: — 66
Overcoming Resistance — 68
   Converting Skeptics Without Bribery — 68
   Manav's Thoughts: — 74
The Final Reflection — 76
   Looking Back Without Falling Over — 76
   Manav's Thoughts: — 81
The Ripple Effect — 82
   Manav's Thoughts: — 85

ACKNOWLEDGMENT

This book is the culmination of countless interactions, experiences, and insights I've gained through an incredible community of Agile practitioners and enthusiasts.

First and foremost, my heartfelt thanks go to all the participants in my Agile workshops and courses. Your questions, arising from the unique challenges of your teams and industries, have been the cornerstone of my growing understanding of Agile methodologies. Whether in software development, marketing, healthcare, or education, your diverse perspectives have led me to explore the versatility of Agile principles and find new, innovative ways to apply them in different contexts. You are the co-creators of this book and have shaped it with every question like "But how can Agile work in our traditional industry?"

A huge thank you goes out to all the teams I have had the honor of coaching and working alongside. As an Agile Coach, Scrum Master, and Product Owner, I have been fortunate to be part of your transformative journeys. Your successes have been my successes, your challenges my learning moments. This book is as much a product of your experiences as it is of my words.

To my clients who had the courage to embark on the path of Agile transformation with me - your trust has been my greatest motivation. Your willingness to question the status quo, embrace change, and relentlessly strive for improvement has been an inexhaustible source of inspiration. The stories in this book reflect your courage and determination.

A very special thank you to my family and friends who patiently endured my endless Agile analogies on a daily basis and supported me through the ups and downs of the writing process. Your love and encouragement were my constant sprint goal.

I'm deeply grateful to the Agile community at large - the thought leaders, practitioners, and innovators who continue to evolve and refine Agile methodologies. Your work has been a constant source of inspiration and learning.

Finally, I would like to thank you, the reader. By choosing to pick up this book, you are taking a step towards better understanding and applying Agile principles. Whether you are a novice or an experienced Agile practitioner, I hope Sally's story resonates with you and enriches your Agile journey.

Thank you all for being part of this incredible Agile adventure. This book was created for you and because of you. Together, we continue to learn, adapt, and improve - truly embodying the Agile spirit.

Chapter 1

The Struggles of Frameworks

When One Size Fits None

Sally McKinnon, WhisperCorp's Agile Coach and designated solver of chaos stared at her cluttered inbox, wondering if it was time to start charging overtime for stress management. Each email subject line seemed to scream louder than the last: "URGENT: Framework Failure," "Scrum Disaster Looming," and the poetic "Help! Scrum is Screwing Us!" She took a long sip of her coffee—third cup? Fourth? The taste didn't matter anymore; caffeine was the lifeblood of her sanity.

"Alright," she muttered, rising from her chair with the enthusiasm of someone heading to jury duty. The morning's cross-team meeting promised fireworks, and not the fun, celebratory kind. Grabbing her notebook and trusty whiteboard markers, she marched toward the conference room, dodging developers slouched over monitors and marketers in animated discussions about font choices. It was just another day in Agile paradise.

Inside the conference room, tension hung heavy. On one side of the table sat Marketing's Scrum team, looking like they'd been served cold coffee. Across from them was the Development Kanban crew, arms folded as if preparing for battle. In the middle sat Product Management, their nervous glances ping-ponging between the two groups.

Sally clapped her hands, summoning her best "game show host" energy. "Who's ready to tackle some inter-team dependencies?"

The room erupted into a cacophony of complaints

"Marketing keeps changing their priorities!"

"Development never sticks to their commitments!"

"Product doesn't understand how either of our frameworks work!"

Sally raised her hands, feeling less like an Agile Coach and more like a referee at a particularly rowdy kindergarten soccer match. "Okay, okay, let's take this one at a time. Marketing, what seems to be the issue?"

Jenna from Marketing wasted no time launching into complaints. "We're trying to maintain stable sprints, but Development keeps dragging our designers into last-minute 'emergencies.' It's impossible to meet our goals when our team's being raided like a cookie jar at a toddler's party."

Before Sally could respond, Raj from Development jumped in. "That's rich coming from you guys! Your 'sprint goals' change so fast that we'd need psychic powers to keep up. We're trying to maintain a steady flow here, but your constant priority shifts are giving us whiplash!"

Product Management's representative, a bespectacled man named Tom, timidly raised his hand. "I think if we could just align our–"

"Not now, Tom!" both sides shouted in unison.

Sally pinched the bridge of her nose, wondering if it was too early for a vacation. Or retirement. As the bickering continued, her mind wandered to the frameworks that were supposed to be solving these problems, not causing them.

Scrum, with its neatly time-boxed sprints and clearly defined roles, was meant to bring order to the chaos of software development. Kanban, with its visual boards and focus on flow, was supposed to streamline processes and reduce bottlenecks. So why did it feel like they were oil and water, refusing to mix no matter how hard they shook the bottle?

As she watched Jenna and Raj engage in a pointing match that would put dueling wizards to shame, Sally had an epiphany. These frameworks, for all their merits, were just tools. And like any tool, they were only as good as the people wielding them.

Sally massaged her temples. This wasn't a meeting; it was a live-action soap opera. With a deep breath, she raised her voice.

"Enough! Let's pause for a second. Everyone, take a step back. What are we really here to do?"

The room fell silent. Somewhere in the distance, the faint hum of a microwave signaled someone committing the unforgivable crime of reheating fish.

Tom finally spoke up, tentative but audible. "Deliver value to customers?"

Sally snapped her fingers. "Exactly! And how do we do that?"

Jenna frowned. "By sticking to our process?"

Raj chimed in, "By keeping our flow consistent?"

Sally shook her head. "Those are means to an end, not the end itself. We deliver value by working together, communicating, by adapting to change. Our frameworks should support that, not hinder it."

She grabbed a marker and approached the whiteboard. "Let's forget the frameworks for a second. Let's map out what's actually happening. Where are the real pain points? Where are we succeeding?"

Markers squeaked as she began sketching a flowchart. The team hesitated at first, but soon they leaned in, pointing out bottlenecks and gaps. What emerged wasn't pretty—a tangled mess resembling spaghetti more than strategy—but it was real. And it was theirs.

"See this?" Sally gestured to a cluster of tasks marked "blocked." "This is where things are breaking down. Now let's figure out why."

As the group discussed their workflow, Sally began drawing parallels to Agile methodologies. "You know," she said, "this part reminds me of Kanban. We're visualizing our process and spotting bottlenecks."

Dave perked up. "Kanban? I thought we were doing Scrum."

Sally chuckled. "Well, we're not doing either, exactly. But both have elements that could be useful for us."

She grabbed a marker and drew two columns on a whiteboard. "Let's think about this. Scrum is all about fixed-length sprints and a set of specific roles and events. It's great for teams that need a lot of structure and have work that can be broken down into sprint-sized chunks."

In the Scrum column, she wrote: "Sprints, Daily Standups, Sprint Planning, Review, Retrospective."

"Kanban, on the other hand," she continued, writing in the second column, "is more flexible. It's all about visualizing work, limiting work in progress, and managing flow. It's often good for teams with a lot of incoming ad-hoc requests or maintenance work."

The team gathered around, intrigued by this impromptu Agile framework lesson.

"But here's the thing," Sally said, capping her marker with a flourish. "We don't have to choose just one. We can take elements from both, or neither, depending on what works for us. The key is to understand our own needs and constraints."

Tom raised his hand tentatively. "So... we're creating our own methodology?"

Sally grinned. "Exactly! Welcome to the world of Agile, folks. Where the frameworks are made up, and the points don't matter!"

The team laughed, the tension in the room dissipating. As they returned to their dependency mapping with renewed energy, Sally couldn't help but feel they were on the verge of something exciting. They weren't just adopting a framework; they were creating something uniquely theirs.

As the meeting wrapped up, Sally felt a mix of exhaustion and exhilaration. They hadn't solved all their problems, not by a long shot, but they'd taken the first step: acknowledging that their current approach wasn't working.

Back at her desk, Sally slumped into her chair, her mind racing. She pulled up the Agile Manifesto on her screen, those four simple value statements that had revolutionized software development. Her eyes lingered on the first line: "Individuals and interactions over processes and tools."

"Well," she muttered to herself, "we've certainly got the 'individuals' part down. Now we just need to work on those 'interactions'."

As if on cue, an email notification popped up. It was from the CEO, subject line: "Need update on Agile transformation ASAP!!!"

Sally groaned, her head thunking onto her desk. She was reminded of something her old mentor used to say: "Agile is simple, but it's not easy." Boy, was that an understatement.

As she lifted her head, her eyes fell on a framed quote on her desk: "Insanity is doing the same thing over and over and expecting different results." She'd always attributed it to Einstein, though she vaguely remembered reading somewhere that he probably never said it. Still, the sentiment rang true.

If they kept trying to force-fit these frameworks without addressing the underlying issues, they'd keep getting the same results. It was time for a new approach.

Sally straightened up, a determined glint in her eye. She opened a new document and typed at the top: "The Sally Model: Because One Size Fits None."

As she began to brainstorm, blending elements of different frameworks with the unique needs of WhisperCorp, she couldn't help but chuckle. If someone had told her a year ago that she'd be creating her own Agile framework, she'd have laughed them out of the room. But here she was, about to embark on a journey that would either revolutionize WhisperCorp's way of working or land her in the unemployment line.

Either way, it was bound to be an interesting ride.

Just as she was hitting her stride, a calendar reminder popped up: "All-hands meeting in 5 minutes."

Sally sighed, saving her document. Rome wasn't built in a day, and neither would the Sally Model. But as she headed towards the meeting room, dodging a Nerf dart war that had broken out in the developer pit (apparently, their own unique way of "resolving conflicts"), she felt a spark of excitement.

Change was coming to WhisperCorp, whether they were ready for it or not. And Sally intended to be the one leading the charge, armed with nothing but a whiteboard marker, a pocket full of sticky notes, and an unshakeable belief that there had to be a better way.

As she pushed open the door to the crowded meeting room, she muttered under her breath, "Buckle up, WhisperCorp. The Sally Model is coming, and it's going to turn this place upside down."

Little did she know just how prophetic those words would prove to be.

Manav's Thoughts:

You know, when I wrote about Sally facing that chaotic cross-team meeting, I was really trying to highlight something I've seen countless times in my consulting work. It's fascinating how teams can be using Agile frameworks, yet still end up in these productivity-killing conflicts.

That moment when Sally realizes they need to go back to Agile values - that's crucial. It's easy to get caught up in the ceremonies and artifacts of Scrum or Kanban, but without a foundation in Agile values, it's all just theater. I've seen teams with beautiful Kanban boards and meticulous sprint planning sessions still fail to deliver value because they've lost sight of what really matters.

The way different teams were blaming each other for delays - that's a classic sign of silos persisting despite Agile implementation. It reminds me of a large financial institution I worked with. They had all the trappings of Agile, but departments were still throwing work "over the wall" to each other. It took months of coaching to break down those invisible barriers.

Sally's inner dialogue about frameworks not being enough to solve their problems - that's a realization I wish more leaders would have earlier in their Agile journey. Frameworks are tools, not solutions. It's like giving someone a hammer and expecting them to build a house. Without understanding the principles of construction (or in our case, Agile values), you're not going to get far.

I'm reminded of a great article by Ron Jeffries, one of the original signatories of the Agile Manifesto, called *"Dark Scrum"*. It talks about how Scrum when implemented without understanding, can actually make things worse. It's a must-read for anyone feeling stuck in their Agile implementation.

That final scene, where Sally decides to take a step back and go to the basics - that's often where the real transformation begins. In my experience, the most successful Agile adoptions are those that start with a deep dive into Agile values and principles, before ever talking about daily stand-ups or story points.

It makes me think of the *Cynefin framework* by Dave Snowden. So many organizations try to apply complicated solutions (like rigid implementations of Scrum) to complex problems. But in complex domains, we need to probe-sense-respond, which is exactly what Sally is setting up to do.

I hope readers take away from this chapter not just the humor, but the underlying message: Agile is not about following a recipe, it's about embracing a mindset of continuous learning and adaptation. And sometimes, that means going back to square one.

Sally's impromptu comparison of Scrum and Kanban touches on a crucial point in Agile adoption: understanding that different methodologies have different strengths and are suited to different contexts.

This kind of comparative analysis is vital when a team is trying to figure out their Agile approach. It's not about finding the "best" methodology, but about finding (or creating) the approach that best fits the team's needs and constraints.

I'm reminded of a software company I once worked with. They started with Scrum, but found that their support team, which dealt with a high volume of unpredictable customer issues, struggled with the sprint structure. By adopting a Kanban approach for the support team while the development team stuck with Scrum, they were able to create a hybrid model that worked much better for their specific context.

For teams looking to dive deeper into different Agile methodologies, I highly recommend "Scrum and XP from the Trenches" by Henrik Kniberg for a practical look at Scrum, and "Kanban: Successful Evolutionary Change for Your Technology Business" by David J. Anderson for Kanban. Both books offer invaluable insights into how these methodologies work in practice.

Remember, the Agile Manifesto values "Individuals and interactions over processes and tools." This means that no framework should be adopted blindly. The best approach is often one that's tailored to the specific needs of the team and organization.

Chapter 2

Embracing Agile Values

Learning to Love Change (Without Therapy)

Sally McKinnon squinted at the Agile Manifesto pinned to her cubicle wall, its words glaring back like an old friend turned stranger. The once-reassuring phrases now seemed to mock her, each one a specter of forgotten ideals. "How did we stray so far?" she murmured, clutching her "World's Okayest Agile Coach" mug as if it might offer counsel.

The coffee inside—a murky brew more sludge than sustenance—coated her tongue with bitterness. Her gaze snagged on the first value: *Individuals and interactions over processes and tools.* She snorted, the sound sharp against the hum of office chatter. At WhisperCorp, it felt like they'd swapped that around—humans reduced to cogs in a well-oiled but soulless machine. On her worst days, she half-expected to find sleek robots at their desks, spouting corporate mantras like, "Let's circle back" or "Can I get that by EOD?"

Her thoughts lingered on yesterday's chaotic cross-team meeting—a hurricane of half-baked ideas and misplaced priorities. Maybe it was time to get back to basics, to remind everyone what Agile was really about. Not with kumbaya hand-holding, but with a clear-eyed look at the "why" behind it all.

Her determination set her ergonomic chair spinning. With a grimace, she adjusted it, muttering, "Note to self: fix settings before attempting dramatic gestures."

Operation: Agile Reality Check was born.

Her first stop: Dave from Development. Dave could bend computers to his will, but put him in front of a whiteboard and he froze like a deer in high beams.

"Hey, Dave," Sally said, leaning on the edge of his cubicle, aiming for casual. "Got a minute?"

Dave's gaze lifted from his screen, his eyes hazy, as if still immersed in code. "Uh, sure. Did I miss a standup?"

"Nope. Just wanted your off-the-record thoughts on how our Agile process is working."

His eyebrows shot up. "Off the record? Sounds suspicious."

"Promise, no traps," Sally said, palms up. "I'm just looking for honesty—the good, the bad, and the 'what were we thinking?'"

Dave leaned back, his chair squeaking in protest. "Well, sometimes it feels like we're following Scrum rules so rigidly we've forgotten the point."

"Go on." Sally nodded encouragingly.

"Like yesterday," he said, warming to the topic. "We had this idea to improve the user interface, but because it wasn't in the sprint backlog, we couldn't act on it. By the next sprint, the moment was gone. It's like…"

"Planning a picnic a month in advance and refusing to adapt when there's a hurricane?" Sally offered.

Dave grinned. "Exactly. Sometimes you need an indoor picnic."

"So," Sally said, "we need to pivot more. Be... agile?"

Dave chuckled. "Revolutionary, right?"

This was what she'd been missing - real, honest conversations about how Agile principles applied in their day-to-day work. Buoyed by their exchange, Sally moved on to Jenna from Marketing. If Dave was a fish climbing a tree, Jenna was a squirrel trying to explain astrophysics—all enthusiasm, little precision.

"Jenna," Sally began, perching on the desk's edge. "If our Agile process were a dinner party, how would you describe it?"

Jenna blinked. "Chaotic? Like everyone brought dessert and no one thought to make a main course?"

Sally laughed. "What if, instead of pre-planned dishes, we brought ingredients and cooked together based on what we had?"

Jenna's eyes widened. "You mean... collaborate?"

"Radical, I know. But isn't that the point of Agile?"

As the day wore on, similar conversations unfolded across departments. Patterns emerged: an over-reliance on rigid frameworks, a lack of cross-team communication, and a disconnect from Agile's core values. By evening, Sally's head swirled with metaphors:

- *We're driving by GPS and ignoring the road ahead.* (Tom from Product Management)
- *We're a football team that knows all the plays but forgot how to play.* (Sarah in QA)
- *We're speaking different dialects and blaming each other for not understanding.* (Brad in Sales, surprisingly insightful!)

Back at her desk, Sally collapsed into her chair, exhilarated yet drained. Her "Sally Model" document glared at her, half-empty. With renewed purpose, she began typing, translating the day's insights into actionable ideas.

Her stomach growled. She glanced at the clock—7:30 PM. Sensible would be going home, eating a proper meal, and tackling this tomorrow. But Sally had never been sensible.

Grinning, she called the local pizza joint. "Large pizza. Half pepperoni, half surprise me. I'm feeling agile tonight."

As she waited for her dinner to arrive, Sally began to type, her ideas flowing faster than she could get them down. The Sally Model was taking shape, built on the foundation of those four simple Agile values, but tailored to the unique needs and quirks of WhisperCorp.

When the pizza arrived, she barely noticed, her focus riveted on her screen. It wasn't until she bit into an unexpected combo—pineapple and bacon—that she paused. "Huh. Not bad."

She jotted a note: *Embrace the unexpected. Sometimes the best solutions come from unlikely combinations.*

The Sally Model was coming to life, one pizza-fueled insight at a time. And if she could get her teams to embrace change as easily as she'd embraced this unexpected pizza topping combination, well... they just might have a chance at turning WhisperCorp's Agile transformation around.

By the time she packed up, her desk was a battlefield of sticky notes and pizza crumbs, the beginnings of what could be a groundbreaking Agile approach—or the ramblings of a caffeine-addled dreamer. Only time would tell. But Sally knew one thing: this journey was just beginning, and it was bound to be one hell of a ride.

Manav's Thoughts:

When I wrote about Sally's one-on-one conversations with team members, I was touching on something I've seen countless times in my consulting work. People's frustrations with Agile often come from a misunderstanding of its core values.

Take Dave, for instance, when he talks about feeling constrained by the framework. That's such a common experience. I've met developers who see Scrum as a straitjacket instead of an empowering structure. This usually happens when Agile is implemented top-down, with a heavy focus on practices but little explanation of the 'why' behind them.

That's why Sally's use of everyday metaphors to explain Agile concepts resonated with me. I've found this approach incredibly effective in my own training sessions. I once compared Agile values to adjusting plans for a family vacation, which helped a client finally grasp the concept of embracing change.

The real magic happens when teams stop viewing Agile as just a work framework and start applying its principles to other areas of life. I once worked with a team lead who used Agile principles for his personal fitness goals. Not only did he lose 30 pounds, but his team's performance improved because he started modeling those principles at work.

This shift—from seeing Agile as a set of practices to understanding it as a mindset—is crucial. It reminds me of the 'Shu Ha Ri' concept in martial arts. First, you follow the rules (Shu), then adapt them (Ha), and eventually transcend them (Ri). This progression is essential to truly embracing Agile values. For those wanting to explore this more, I highly recommend *The Agile Samurai* by Jonathan Rasmusson—it's an excellent resource.

Sally's impromptu analysis of WhisperCorp's work environment illustrates a vital but often-overlooked step in Agile transformations: understanding the current state before attempting change.

This kind of organizational assessment is like navigating a ship. Without knowing your starting point, it's impossible to chart a course to your destination. Tools like Value Stream Mapping are incredibly useful here—they help teams visualize workflows and identify bottlenecks.

I'm reminded of a financial services company I worked with. They were excited to adopt Scrum, but when we mapped their current processes, we uncovered significant inter-departmental dependencies. Their biggest challenges weren't things Scrum could solve alone. This kind of discovery is why assessing the current state is so important.

If you're interested in diving deeper into this topic, I recommend *The Phoenix Project* by Gene Kim. It's a novel that brilliantly demonstrates how systemic issues in organizations impact workflows and how Lean and Agile principles can help address them.

It's important to remember that the goal of these assessments isn't to assign blame or point fingers. Instead, it's about creating a shared understanding of the current reality. Only then can teams envision a better future state and take actionable steps to get there.

Sally's realization about the Agile mindset ties all of this together. Too often, organizations focus on implementing Agile practices without truly embracing the mindset. It's like buying exercise equipment without actually using it.

The Agile mindset is about embracing uncertainty, prioritizing value delivery, and continuously learning and improving. It requires a shift from a plan-driven approach to an adaptive one.

I've seen this firsthand with a tech company that struggled to adopt Agile. They had the ceremonies in place but were still operating with a traditional, plan-driven mindset. The real breakthrough came when we focused on cultivating an Agile mindset across the organization.

For those who want to explore the Agile mindset further, I highly recommend *Mindset: The New Psychology of Success* by Carol S. Dweck. It's not specifically about Agile, but its insights into the power of a growth mindset align perfectly with Agile thinking.

Adopting an Agile mindset isn't a one-time change—it's an ongoing journey. It takes constant reflection, a willingness to challenge

assumptions, and a commitment to improving how we work and think.

Chapter 3

Mapping Dependencies

Untangling the Corporate Spaghetti

Sally McKinnon stood before the whiteboard, marker in hand, feeling like a conductor about to lead a very reluctant orchestra through a particularly challenging symphony. The conference room was packed with representatives from every department, each eyeing the others with a mix of suspicion and resignation.

"Alright, folks," Sally began, injecting as much enthusiasm into her voice as she could muster at 9 AM on a Monday. "Today, we're going to map out our dependencies. Think of it as creating a family tree, but instead of relatives, we're charting how our work flows—or doesn't flow—across departments."

Dave from Development raised his hand. "Is this going to be like that trust fall exercise from last year's team building? Because I still have trust issues after Marketing dropped me."

Jenna from Marketing shot him a glare. "That was one time, Dave. Let it go."

Sally chuckled, remembering the ill-fated attempt at team bonding. "No trust falls today, I promise. This is about understanding how our work impacts each other. Think of it as... detective work. We're CSI: WhisperCorp, and we're solving the case of the Mysterious Workflow Bottlenecks."

As Sally began drawing boxes on the whiteboard, representing different teams and processes, she couldn't help but feel like she was creating some sort of deranged flowchart of office politics. It was less "A leads to B" and more "A grudgingly acknowledges B's existence while secretly wishing C would just disappear."

"Okay," Sally said, turning back to the group. "Let's start with Product Management. Tom, can you walk us through your process for defining new features?"

Tom, a bespectacled man who always looked slightly startled, stood up. "Well, we start by gathering requirements from stakeholders, then we prioritize—"

"That's the problem right there!" Dave interrupted. "You prioritize without consulting us about technical feasibility. Remember the 'flying car' feature request?"

Sally raised an eyebrow. "Flying car feature?"

Jenna sighed. "It was a metaphor, Dave. The stakeholder wanted a 'revolutionary' new interface."

"A metaphor that wasted two weeks of development time!" Dave shot back.

Sally quickly drew a jagged line between the Product Management and Development boxes, labeling it "Communication breakdown - metaphor malfunction."

"Okay, okay," she said, trying to keep the peace. "So we've identified our first issue: Product Management needs to consult with Development earlier in the process. Tom, how do you feel about that?"

Tom nodded slowly. "I suppose we could... but then Marketing always comes in at the last minute with 'urgent' requests that throw off our entire roadmap."

Jenna bristled. "That's because Sales keeps promising features we haven't even heard of!"

Sally's marker squeaked across the whiteboard as she frantically tried to keep up with the volley of accusations. By the time everyone had aired their grievances, the once-neat flowchart looked more like a plate of spaghetti that had been struck by lightning.

Stepping back, Sally surveyed the chaos on the board. It was a mess, but it was an honest mess. For the first time, they were seeing the full picture of how their work impacted each other.

"Folks," Sally said, her voice cutting through the murmur of discontent. "Look at this board. What do you see?"

"A Jackson Pollock painting?" quipped Sarah from QA.

"Close," Sally grinned. "It's a visualization of our current process. Or lack thereof. But here's the thing—this mess? It's the first step towards fixing our problems. We can't improve what we can't see, and now we're seeing it all."

The room fell silent as everyone contemplated the tangle of lines and boxes.

"So... what do we do now?" Dave asked, his voice uncharacteristically subdued.

Sally capped her marker with a flourish. "Now, we start untangling. One strand at a time."

Over the next few hours, Sally guided the team through a series of exercises designed to identify the key bottlenecks and communication breakdowns. It wasn't always pretty—at one point, she had to physically stand between Dave and Brad from Sales to prevent a whiteboard marker duel—but slowly, surely, progress was made.

As lunch approached, Sally called for a break. "Great work, everyone. When we come back, we'll start brainstorming solutions."

As the room emptied, Sally slumped into a chair, exhausted but exhilarated. She pulled out her notebook, jotting down ideas for her evolving framework.

"The Sally Model," she muttered as she wrote.

> **Rule #1:** *Visualize the mess before you can clean it up.*

Just then, Tom from Product Management approached, looking sheepish. "Sally, I wanted to apologize for getting defensive earlier. I never realized how much our decisions impacted the other teams."

Sally smiled warmly. "That's the beauty of this exercise, Tom. It's not about pointing fingers; it's about understanding. Transparency isn't always comfortable, but it's necessary."

Tom nodded thoughtfully. "It's like... when my wife and I first moved in together. We had to have some awkward conversations about our habits before we could figure out how to live together harmoniously."

"Exactly!" Sally exclaimed. "Agile is all about that kind of transparency and continuous improvement. We're not just coworkers; we're in a relationship with each other's work."

As Tom walked away, looking slightly less bewildered than usual, Sally turned back to her notes.

> **Rule #2:** *Treat your team like a relationship - communicate often, be honest, and always replace the toilet paper roll when it's empty.*

The afternoon session brought more breakthroughs as the team started to identify potential solutions to their workflow issues. Ideas flew back and forth across the room like a game of ping pong.

"What if we had weekly cross-team syncs?" suggested Jenna.

"And a shared backlog that everyone can see?" added Dave.

"Ooh, and a 'no metaphor' rule for feature requests," Sarah chimed in, shooting a playful glance at Tom.

Sally's marker danced across the whiteboard, capturing each idea. The mess from the morning was slowly transforming into something that, while not quite orderly, at least had a sense of purpose.

As the session wound down, Sally felt a buzz of excitement in the room. People were talking animatedly, making plans to follow up with each other. The silos that had seemed so impenetrable that morning were showing cracks.

"Alright, team," Sally said, calling for attention. "We've made incredible progress today. We've shed light on our issues, and now we have a roadmap for addressing them. Remember, this is just the beginning. Continuous improvement is a journey, not a destination."

As the team filed out, chattering excitedly, Sally turned back to the whiteboard. She erased a section and quickly sketched out a rough diagram of her emerging framework. At the center, she wrote

"Transparency" and drew arrows connecting it to "Communication," "Collaboration," and "Continuous Improvement."

"The Sally Model," she mused. "A framework for turning office chaos into coordinated symphony. Or at least a less chaotic jazz improvisation."

Just then, her phone buzzed with a message from her boss: "Heard about your dependency mapping session. Sounds intense. Everything okay?"

Sally grinned as she typed her reply: "More than okay. We're finally seeing the forest AND the trees. And we're planting seeds for a whole new ecosystem."

As she packed up her things, Sally couldn't help but feel a sense of pride. Today had been challenging, messy, and at times frustrating, but it had also been a huge step forward. They had embraced transparency, faced their issues head-on, and come out stronger for it.

Walking to her car, Sally's mind was already racing with ideas for the next phase of her framework.

Rule #3: *Embrace the mess, find the patterns, and always keep a sense of humor.*

Oh, and stock up on whiteboard markers. You're gonna need them.

As she drove home, the setting sun painting the sky in vibrant hues, Sally couldn't help but feel optimistic. WhisperCorp was on the brink of something big, something transformative. And she, armed with nothing but a marker, a whiteboard, and an ever-evolving framework, was leading the charge.

The Sally Model was taking shape, one chaotic, transparent, continuously improving step at a time. And Sally McKinnon, Agile Coach extraordinaire, was ready for whatever challenges tomorrow might bring.

As long as it didn't involve trust falls. Some things, even Agile couldn't fix.

Manav's Thoughts:

This chapter's dependency mapping session is based on a technique I've used countless times, inspired by Lean's value stream mapping. It's always fascinating how making work visible can be both uncomfortable and enlightening for teams.

Take the moment when Sally draws that "jagged line" between Product Management and Development, labeling it "Communication breakdown – metaphor malfunction." It's such a striking example. So often, what teams think of as a process issue turns out to be a communication problem instead. I once worked with a company where simply improving how user stories were written solved about 50% of their delivery challenges!

There's something incredibly powerful when a team sees the full picture of their work for the first time. I've facilitated sessions where people who've worked together for years suddenly gain a clear understanding of what their colleagues actually do. That realization? It's a real 'aha' moment.

Sally's rule about visualizing the mess before trying to clean it up is spot on. It ties right back to Lean's principle of 'bringing problems to the surface.' A fantastic illustration of this concept is in *The Phoenix Project*.

I also love the idea of treating cross-functional collaboration like a relationship. It's an approach I've found incredibly effective. Patrick Lencioni's work on team dynamics, especially *The Five Dysfunctions of a Team*, is a go-to reference for me when coaching teams on working better together.

If there's one takeaway from this chapter, I hope it's this: transparency and visualization aren't just nice-to-have Agile practices. They're foundational for building shared understanding and fostering real collaboration.

Chapter 4

Cross-Team Collaboration

Herding Cats Across Department Lines

Sally McKinnon stood in the conference room, surveying the scene before her with a mix of anticipation and trepidation. The room was set up for what she had optimistically dubbed "The Great WhisperCorp Collaboration Extravaganza," but at the moment, it looked more like a middle school dance where no one wanted to be the first on the dance floor.

Representatives from every department were scattered around the room, clumped together in their usual groupings. The developers huddled in one corner, furiously tapping away at their laptops. The marketing team was busy rebranding the event on their phones, probably coming up with catchy hashtags like #CollaborateOrDie. Meanwhile, the sales team looked like they were strategizing how to sell the idea of collaboration to everyone else.

Sally took a deep breath. "Alright, folks!" she announced, getting everyone's attention. "Welcome to our cross-functional workshop. Today, we're going to break down some walls, build some bridges, and hopefully not end up with a Tower of Babel situation."

She was met with a sea of blank stares and a few nervous chuckles.

"Tough crowd," Sally muttered under her breath before continuing with renewed enthusiasm. "Let's kick things off with a little icebreaker. I want you all to pair up with someone from a different department and share the strangest customer request you've ever received."

There was a moment of hesitation before people slowly, reluctantly began to mingle. Sally watched as Dave from Development approached Jenna from Marketing with all the enthusiasm of a man walking to the gallows.

"So," Dave began awkwardly, "the strangest customer request I ever got was to make our app 'more blue'. Not a specific shade of blue, just... more blue."

Jenna snorted. "That's nothing. We once had a client ask us to make our logo 'more synergistic with the cosmic energy of the universe.'"

Dave's eyes widened. "What does that even mean?"

"Your guess is as good as mine," Jenna shrugged. "We ended up adding a swirl to the logo and called it a day."

As Sally circulated the room, she overheard more bizarre stories being shared, punctuated by laughter and exclamations of disbelief. The ice was beginning to thaw, and people were actually... talking to each other? It was like watching a nature documentary where two different species unexpectedly start to coexist.

"Alright, everyone!" Sally called out after a few minutes. "Now that we've all bonded over the weirdness of our jobs, let's dive into why we're really here. We're going to tackle a hypothetical project together, applying our various expertise to create something amazing."

She unveiled a large whiteboard with a project outline scrawled across it: "Design and launch a new feature: The WhisperBot 3000 - An AI assistant that can read your mind and anticipate your needs."

"Now," Sally continued, barely suppressing a grin, "I know what you're thinking. 'Sally, that's impossible!' And you're right. But that's the beauty of it. We're going to work together to turn this ridiculous idea into something feasible, practical, and actually valuable to our customers."

The room buzzed with a mixture of confusion, amusement, and the faint scent of marker fumes.

"Let's break into cross-functional teams," Sally instructed. "I want to see developers working with marketers, sales collaborating with product management, and QA keeping everyone honest. Remember, there are no bad ideas... except maybe mind-reading AI. That's probably a bad one."

As the teams formed and began to brainstorm, Sally circulated the room, eavesdropping on conversations and offering guidance where needed. She paused near one group where Tom from Product Management was engaged in a heated debate with Sarah from QA.

"But how can we test something that's supposed to read minds?" Sarah was asking, her voice tinged with exasperation.

Tom scratched his head. "Maybe we could... I don't know, hire a psychic to validate the results?"

Sally decided it was time to intervene. "Guys, remember, we're not actually building a mind-reading AI. What's the core problem we're trying to solve here?"

The group fell silent, pondering the question. Finally, Dave spoke up. "I think... we're trying to make our product more intuitive, right? To anticipate user needs before they even realize they have them?"

"Exactly!" Sally beamed. "So how can we achieve that without resorting to supernatural powers?"

The ideas started flowing thick and fast. "We could analyze user behavior patterns," suggested Jenna.

"And use machine learning to predict common user journeys," added Dave.

"Ooh, and we could integrate with calendar apps to anticipate scheduling needs," chimed in Tom.

Sally nodded encouragingly. "Now you're cooking with gas! See how much more we can achieve when we combine our different perspectives?"

As she moved on to the next group, Sally couldn't help but feel a sense of pride. The room was buzzing with energy, ideas were flying back and forth, and people who normally barely acknowledged each other's existence were now engaged in animated discussions.

Of course, it wasn't all smooth sailing. At one point, Sally had to mediate a heated argument between Brad from Sales and Dave over whether "Make it go viral" was a valid technical specification. (Spoiler alert: it wasn't.)

"Brad," Sally said gently, "I appreciate your enthusiasm, but 'going viral' isn't something we can just program. It's a result, not a feature."

Brad looked crestfallen. "But how will we get millions of users without it going viral?"

Dave rolled his eyes. "Maybe by building something that actually works and solves a real problem?"

Sally held up her hands. "You're both right, in a way. Brad, your job is to understand what our customers really need and communicate that to the team. Dave, your job is to figure out how to build it. It's not about going viral; it's about creating value. If we do that right, the users will come."

As the workshop progressed, Sally noticed a shift in the room's dynamics. The invisible walls between departments were starting to crumble. People were exchanging contact info, making plans to follow up on ideas, and even laughing at each other's jokes (even the terrible developer puns that usually only got groans).

Towards the end of the day, Sally gathered everyone for a final debrief. "Alright, team, let's hear what you've come up with."

The presentations that followed were a far cry from the mind-reading AI they had started with. Instead, the teams had come up with practical, innovative ideas that leveraged their combined expertise. There was an AI-powered personal assistant that learned from user behavior, a predictive analytics tool for businesses, and even a smart home integration that had nothing to do with mind reading but everything to do with anticipating user needs.

"I am blown away," Sally said, and she meant it. "Look at what you've accomplished in just one day of real collaboration. Imagine what we could do if we worked like this all the time."

As the teams dispersed, chattering excitedly about their ideas, Sally stayed behind to clean up. She erased the whiteboard, replacing the original project outline with a new note:

> **Rule #4:** *Collaboration is like a potluck dinner. Everyone brings something different to the table, and together, you create a feast.*

Just then, Dave approached her, looking thoughtful. "You know, Sally, I hate to admit it, but this wasn't terrible. I actually learned a lot from working with the other teams."

Sally grinned. "High praise indeed, coming from you. Any particular insights?"

Dave nodded. "Yeah, actually. I realized that when Jenna from Marketing talks about 'user experience,' she's not just saying buzzwords. She really understands how people interact with our product in ways I hadn't even considered."

"And let me guess," Sally added, "she probably learned that some of her 'simple requests' aren't so simple from a development standpoint?"

"Exactly," Dave chuckled. "I think we both gained some perspective today."

As Dave left, Sally added another note to her growing list of Sally Model rules:

Rule #5: *Empathy is the secret ingredient in great collaboration. Walk a mile in each other's shoes, or at least try them on for size.*

Packing up her things, Sally couldn't help but feel a sense of accomplishment. Today had been a big step forward in breaking down the silos that had plagued WhisperCorp for so long. It wasn't perfect – Rome wasn't built in a day, and neither was cross-functional collaboration – but it was progress.

As she walked to her car, Sally's phone buzzed with a notification. It was a company-wide email from the CEO: "Heard great things about today's workshop. Looking forward to seeing how this collaboration translates into results. Keep up the good work!"

Sally smiled to herself. The Sally Model was evolving, shaped by the real-world challenges and triumphs of the WhisperCorp team. It wasn't just about processes or methodologies anymore. It was about people – how they worked together, how they communicated, how they created value.

As she drove home, the setting sun painting the sky in vibrant hues, Sally's mind was already racing with ideas for the next phase of her

Agile transformation journey. Breaking down silos was just the beginning. Now, they needed to build something new in their place – a truly collaborative, adaptive, and value-driven organization.

But first, she needed sleep. And coffee. Lots and lots of coffee. Because tomorrow was another day in the wonderful, wacky world of Agile at WhisperCorp, and Sally McKinnon was ready for whatever challenges it might bring.

As long as it didn't involve mind-reading AI. Some ideas, even Agile couldn't salvage.

Manav's Thoughts:

The "Great WhisperCorp Collaboration Extravaganza" scene really shows the awkwardness and potential of cross-functional collaboration. I've had many such sessions, and that initial discomfort is so authentic. It's like watching a nature documentary where different species are forced to coexist.

The icebreaker about strange customer requests is a technique I've used countless times. It's amazing how shared humor can break down barriers. I once had a team bond over a story about a client who wanted their app to predict the weather based on cat behavior. Absurdity can be a great equalizer!

When Sally introduces the ridiculous "WhisperBot 3000" project, she's employing a strategy I love: using an impossible scenario to foster creativity. It's similar to the "worst idea" brainstorming technique, where teams intentionally come up with bad ideas to lower the barrier for sharing and then pivot to practical solutions.

The scene where Brad from Sales and Dave argue over whether "Make it go viral" is a valid technical specification. I've mediated countless discussions between technical and non-technical team members. It's crucial to create a shared language and understanding.

Sally's realization about how Agile principles apply to her personal life is an epiphany I've seen many professionals have – when Agile truly becomes a mindset rather than just a work methodology.

The addition of "Empathy is the secret ingredient in great collaboration" to the Sally Model rules on precise. It echoes the work of Nonviolent Communication by Marshall Rosenberg, which I recommend to teams struggling with collaboration.

For readers wanting to dive deeper into cross-functional collaboration, I also suggest you pick up "Team Topologies" by Matthew Skelton and Manuel Pais. It provides excellent insights into team interactions and cognitive load in software delivery.

Chapter 5

Introducing Custom Sprints

Racing at Your Own Pace

Sally McKinnon stood before the WhisperCorp development team, feeling like a mad scientist about to unleash a new creation upon the world. "Alright, folks," she announced, barely containing her excitement, "today, we're going to shake things up. We're going to create our very own custom sprint!"

Dave, the lead developer, raised an eyebrow. "Custom sprint? Is that like when I try to customize my sandwich at Subway and end up with a monstrosity that not even my dog will eat?"

Sally chuckled. "Close, but with fewer regrettable food choices. We're going to take elements from Scrum, sprinkle in some Kanban magic, and create a process that works specifically for us."

The team exchanged nervous glances. They'd gotten comfortable with their current process, imperfect as it was. Change was scary, like trying a new hairstyle or switching from coffee to tea (the horror!).

"Don't worry," Sally reassured them, sensing their apprehension. "Think of it as an experiment. We're scientists in the lab of Agile, and our hypothesis is that we can create a better way of working. And if we blow something up along the way, well, that's just part of the scientific process, right?"

Jenna from Marketing piped up, "As long as we don't blow up the coffee machine, I'm in."

As Sally introduced the concept of custom sprints, she found herself reflecting on the thought process that led her to this point.

"You know," she said, addressing the team, "when I first started thinking about our custom approach, I realized we needed to strike a balance. We need enough structure to keep us focused and aligned, but enough flexibility to adapt to our unique challenges."

She grabbed a marker and started sketching on the whiteboard. "Think of it like building a custom car. We're not just picking a car off the lot; we're selecting the components that work best for us."

The team leaned in, intrigued by the analogy.

"Our engine," Sally continued, drawing a simple car outline, "that's our core values. Things like transparency, continuous improvement, and delivering value to our customers. That's what drives us forward."

She added wheels to her drawing. "The wheels, those are our practices. Daily stand-ups, regular planning sessions, retrospectives. They keep us moving smoothly."

"But here's the important part," she said, her voice taking on a more serious tone. "The driver? That's us. We decide where this car goes. We adjust our course based on what we learn along the way."

Dave nodded slowly. "So we're not just following a prescribed route. We're... navigating our own path?"

"Exactly!" Sally beamed. "We're creating a methodology that fits us, not trying to fit ourselves into a framework that already exists."

As the team began discussing how they could shape their custom sprints, Sally felt a surge of excitement. They weren't just adopting Agile; they were making it their own.

And so began WhisperCorp's great Agile experiment. Sally introduced the concept of dynamic Work in Progress (WIP) limits, explaining it was like a buffet where you could only put three items on your plate at a time. "But," she added with a mischievous grin, "unlike a real buffet, you can adjust your plate size based on how hungry you are."

The team decided to start with a two-week sprint cycle but with the flexibility to adjust it in real-time based on feedback. "Think of it as a road trip," Sally explained. "We have a destination in mind, but if we find a cool attraction along the way, we can make a detour."

As they embarked on their first custom sprint, chaos ensued. It was amusing, slightly painful to watch, but ultimately fascinating.

On day three, Sally found Dave staring at the Kanban board, his eyes glazed over. "Dave? You okay there, buddy?"

Dave turned to her, a wild look in his eyes. "I think I've been staring at this board for so long, the sticky notes are starting to move on their own. Is that normal?"

Sally patted him on the shoulder. "Perfectly normal. It's either Agile magic or sleep deprivation. Possibly both."

Meanwhile, Jenna was having her own crisis. "Sally!" she called out in panic. "I can't move this task to 'In Progress' because of the WIP limit, but I also can't not start it because the client is breathing down my neck. What do I do?"

Sally thought for a moment. "Welcome to the wonderful world of prioritization, Jenna. You have to decide which one needs you most urgently."

"But they're all urgent!" Jenna wailed.

"Ah," Sally nodded sagely, "but are they all important? Remember, urgent is not always important, and important is not always urgent. It's like when your phone buzzes with a notification – it feels urgent, but is it really more important than the task you're already working on?"

As the days progressed, the team slowly began to find their rhythm. They started to see the benefits of limiting their work in progress, realizing that focusing on fewer tasks at a time actually made them more productive. It was like discovering that walking was faster than trying to run while juggling flaming torches.

In their daily stand-ups, which Sally had rebranded as "The Daily Dish" (because who doesn't love a good pun?), the team started to communicate more effectively. They weren't just listing off tasks; they were having real conversations about blockers and opportunities for collaboration.

One morning, Tom from Product Management had a breakthrough. "You know," he said, his eyes wide with revelation, "I think I finally understand what 'maximizing work not done' means. It's not about being lazy; it's about being smart with our efforts!"

Sally beamed like a proud parent. "Exactly, Tom! It's like Marie Kondo-ing our backlog. Does this task spark joy... or in this case value for our customers?"

As they approached the end of their first custom sprint, Sally called the team together for a retrospective. "Alright, gang," she said, uncapping a fresh whiteboard marker, "let's talk about what worked, what didn't, and what made us want to throw our computers out the window."

The discussion that followed was lively, punctuated by laughter, groans, and the occasional facepalm. They talked about the challenges of adapting to dynamic WIP limits, the benefits of more frequent communication, and the unexpected joy of actually finishing tasks before starting new ones.

"I have to admit," Dave said, looking slightly sheepish, "I was skeptical about this whole custom sprint thing. But being able to adjust our process on the fly? That's been... well, pretty awesome actually."

Jenna nodded enthusiastically. "And the focus on finishing things? I feel like I've actually accomplished something, instead of just spinning my wheels."

Sally listened, taking notes and feeling a warmth spread through her chest. This was what Agile was all about – continuous improvement, adapting to change, and most importantly, empowering the team to find better ways of working.

As the retrospective wound down, Sally added a new rule to her ever-growing list of Sally Model principles:

Rule #6: *Your process should fit you, not the other way around.*

It's like finding the perfect pair of jeans – it might take some trying on and adjusting, but when you find the right fit, it's magic.

The team left the room buzzing with ideas for their next sprint. They were energized, excited, and most importantly, they felt ownership over their process. It wasn't Scrum or Kanban or any other predefined framework – it was theirs.

Later that evening, as Sally was packing up to leave, she found a sticky note on her desk. It read: "Thanks for helping us find our Agile groove. We're not perfect, but we're getting better every day. P.S. Dave says thanks for not making us do trust falls."

Sally chuckled, tucking the note into her notebook. As she walked to her car, she reflected on the progress they'd made. They'd taken elements from different Agile methodologies, experimented, failed, learned, and ultimately created something uniquely suited to their needs. It wasn't perfect, but it was theirs, and it was evolving.

The Sally Model was taking shape, not as a rigid framework, but as a flexible, adaptable approach to continuous improvement. It was about empowering teams to experiment, learn, and grow. It was about finding the right balance between structure and flexibility, between process and people.

As she drove home, Sally's mind was already racing with ideas for the next phase of their Agile journey. They'd made great strides in improving their process, but there was still work to be done in cultivating the right mindset and culture.

But that was a challenge for another day. For now, Sally was content with the progress they'd made. They'd taken a leap into the unknown, embraced the chaos, and come out stronger on the other side.

As she pulled into her driveway, Sally's phone buzzed with a message from Dave: "Hey Sally, quick question – for our next sprint, do you think we could implement a 'no meetings Wednesday' rule? My brain needs a break from all this collaboration."

Sally laughed out loud. "Baby steps, Dave," she typed back. "Let's master our custom sprints first. But I'll add it to the backlog... right after 'Install nap pods in the office'."

As she hit send, Sally couldn't help but smile. The road ahead was long, and undoubtedly filled with more challenges, but she was excited for the journey. After all, in the world of Agile, the destination was never as important as the journey itself.

And what a journey it was turning out to be.

Manav's Thoughts:

The chaos that ensues when the team starts experimenting with custom sprints is something many teams go through. Like watching a group of kids learn to ride bikes – there are going to be some scraped knees, but the excitement is palpable.

When Dave stares at the Kanban board, convinced the sticky notes are moving on their own, it humorously reflects a real phenomenon: **information overload**. Teams get so caught up in their new processes that they lose sight of the actual work. It's a reminder of the importance of simplicity in Agile.

Jenna's struggle with WIP limits—and her exasperated cry of "I can't not start it!"—is a scenario we've all encountered. It's a pivotal moment when teams begin to grasp the value of focus and the high cost of context-switching. Joel Spolsky's article, *"Human Task Switches Considered Harmful,"* explores this concept in depth, offering valuable insights into why multitasking can be so detrimental.

Watching a team gradually embrace the benefits of limiting work in progress is inspiring. It's like seeing someone unlock a hidden superpower. Donald Reinertsen's *"The Principles of Product Development Flow"* provides a scientific foundation for many of these Agile practices, illuminating why they work so effectively.

Sally's creative application of Agile principles in her personal life, such as her kitchen Kanban, is something I encourage everyone to try. Personal Kanban, as introduced by Jim Benson, can be a transformative tool for boosting productivity and achieving work-life balance.

The addition of "Your process should fit you, not the other way around" to Sally's rules is a critical insight. It aligns perfectly with the Agile principle of valuing individuals and interactions over processes and tools. I often recommend the *"Agile Fluency Model"* by Diana Larsen and James Shore, which frames Agile adoption as a journey rather than a fixed destination.

The team's enthusiasm for their custom sprint process is infectious. It brings to mind Mihaly Csikszentmihalyi's concept of "flow," where engagement and productivity soar when teams find their rhythm.

Sally's car analogy for designing a custom Agile approach beautifully illustrates the balance between structure and flexibility. This concept, often referred to as "Agile tailoring" in the industry, emphasizes adapting Agile principles to fit specific contexts rather than rigidly adhering to predefined methodologies.

I recall working with a marketing agency that struggled with traditional Scrum because their campaign-based work didn't align with fixed sprints. We developed a hybrid approach, combining Kanban's workflow visualization and WIP limits with key Scrum elements like regular planning and review sessions. This tailored methodology met their unique needs perfectly.

For teams seeking to develop their own Agile approach, I highly recommend Lyssa Adkins' *"Coaching Agile Teams."* It offers invaluable guidance on understanding Agile principles and applying them in diverse contexts.

The goal isn't to craft a flawless methodology from the outset. Instead, focus on creating a framework that works for your team today, with the understanding that it will evolve as you learn and grow. This mindset reflects the Agile principle of responding to change over following a rigid plan.

Above all, keep the essence of Agile at the core of your approach: delivering value swiftly, adapting to change, and continuously improving. These principles ensure your methodology remains effective and aligned with your team's needs.

Chapter 6

Customer-Focused Innovation

Mind Reading for Beginners

Sally McKinnon stood in front of the whiteboard, marker in hand, feeling like a detective piecing together clues in a particularly complex murder mystery. Except instead of solving a crime, she was trying to decipher the cryptic and often contradictory feedback from WhisperCorp's customers.

"Alright, team," she said, turning to face the bleary-eyed group assembled before her. "We've got a challenge ahead of us. We need to take all this customer feedback and turn it into something actually useful. It's like trying to make a gourmet meal out of whatever's left in your fridge the day before you go grocery shopping."

Dave, the lead developer, raised his hand. "Quick question: can we just ignore all the feedback and build whatever we want? It would be so much easier."

Sally chuckled. "Ah, the dream of every developer. Unfortunately, Dave, that's not how this works. Remember, we're here to satisfy the customer, not our own egos... no matter how magnificent those egos might be."

Jenna from Marketing piped up, "But Sally, have you seen some of this feedback? One customer wants our app to make coffee, while another thinks it should predict the stock market. How are we supposed to make sense of all this?"

Sally nodded sympathetically. "I know it seems overwhelming. Think of it like planning a family reunion dinner. Aunt Edna wants vegan options, Uncle Bob insists on meat at every meal, and your cousin's kids will only eat dinosaur-shaped chicken nuggets. Our job is to create a menu that keeps everyone reasonably happy without losing our minds in the process."

The team laughed, the tension in the room easing slightly. Sally continued, "We're going to use this feedback to design our first prototype. Remember, in Agile, we welcome changing requirements. It's not about getting it perfect the first time; it's about learning and adapting."

And so began WhisperCorp's journey into customer-centric prototyping. Sally divided the team into smaller groups, each tasked with tackling a different aspect of the product based on the feedback they'd received.

As the days progressed, Sally found herself bouncing between teams, offering guidance, cracking jokes, and occasionally playing referee when disagreements arose. It was like being a camp counselor for a bunch of overly caffeinated tech enthusiasts.

One afternoon, she found Tom from Product Management staring at his computer screen, a look of utter bewilderment on his face.

"Everything okay there, Tom?" Sally asked, peering over his shoulder.

Tom turned to her, his eyes wide. "Sally, I've been going through the customer feedback for the user interface. Half of them want it simpler, the other half want more features. How am I supposed to make a decision?"

Sally pondered for a moment. "You know, Tom, this reminds me of when I was planning my wedding. My mom wanted a big, traditional affair, while my partner wanted to elope. In the end, we found a middle ground – a small ceremony with close family and friends."

Tom looked at her, confusion evident on his face. "That's great, Sally, but how does that help me with the user interface?"

Sally grinned. "The point is, sometimes you can't make everyone 100% happy. Your job is to find the sweet spot that satisfies the most important needs. Start with the bare essentials that everyone agrees on, then add features in a way that doesn't clutter the main interface. Think of it as a wedding buffet – provide options, but don't force everyone to pile everything on their plate."

As Tom nodded slowly, a glimmer of understanding in his eyes, Sally made a mental note.

> **Rule #7:** *Customer feedback is like a buffet. Take what's valuable, leave what's not, and don't be afraid to go back for seconds on the really good stuff.*

Meanwhile, in another corner of the office, Jenna and Dave were locked in a heated debate about a feature that customers had requested.

"But the customers specifically asked for a button that automatically generates marketing copy!" Jenna insisted, waving a feedback report in the air.

Dave ran a hand through his hair in frustration. "Jenna, we can't just magically create an AI that writes perfect marketing copy. It's not technically feasible... at least not without selling our souls to some very questionable tech giants."

Sally approached cautiously, feeling the eggshells she was walking on. "Okay, folks, let's take a step back. Jenna, can you tell me why the customers are asking for this feature?"

Jenna took a deep breath. "They're struggling to create consistent messaging across their marketing materials. It's time-consuming and often leads to inconsistencies."

Sally nodded. "And Dave, from a technical standpoint, what could we realistically build that might address this need?"

Dave thought for a moment. "Well, we could create a template system with customizable fields. It wouldn't write the copy for them, but it could ensure consistency and save time."

"Great!" Sally exclaimed. "See? We're not ignoring the customer's need; we're just finding a different way to address it. Remember, folks, it's not about building exactly what the customer asks for; it's about solving their underlying problem."

As Jenna and Dave began to sketch out ideas for the template system, Sally added another note to her growing list of Sally Model principles:

> **Rule #8**: *Listen to the problem behind the request. Customers might ask for a fish, but what they really need is a fishing rod."*

The days flew by in a whirlwind of sticky notes, whiteboard diagrams, and an alarming amount of coffee consumption. Sally watched with pride as the team navigated the choppy waters of customer feedback, making decisions, pivoting when necessary, and slowly but surely shaping their prototype.

There were moments of frustration, like when the team realized they'd have to scrap a feature they'd spent days working on because new feedback rendered it obsolete. But there were also moments of triumph, like when they presented an early version of the prototype to a focus group and received overwhelmingly positive responses.

As they approached the end of their prototyping phase, Sally called the team together for a retrospective. "Alright, gang," she said, uncapping her trusty whiteboard marker, "let's talk about what we've learned from this customer-centric approach."

The discussion that followed was lively and insightful. Team members shared stories of challenges they'd overcome, lessons they'd learned, and insights they'd gained into their customers' needs.

"I have to admit," Dave said, a note of surprise in his voice, "I was skeptical about all this customer feedback stuff at first. But seeing how our decisions actually solved real problems for real people... it's pretty cool."

Jenna nodded enthusiastically. "And the way we were able to adapt our plans based on new information? It felt so much more... I don't know, alive than our old way of working."

Sally beamed, feeling a warm glow of pride. This was what Agile was all about – responding to change, delivering value, and putting the customer at the heart of everything.

As the retrospective wound down, Sally added a new rule to her list:

Rule #9: *Your product is like a garden. Plant the seeds your customers need, water it with their feedback, and don't be afraid to prune when necessary.*

Later that evening, as Sally was packing up to leave, she found herself reflecting on the progress they'd made. They'd taken a jumble of conflicting customer feedback and turned it into a prototype that actually solved real problems. It wasn't perfect – no first prototype ever is – but it was a huge step in the right direction.

As she walked to her car, Sally's phone buzzed with a message from her partner: "Don't forget, we're hosting game night tonight. Your cousin's bringing her new vegan boyfriend, and your uncle insists on having his 'special' chili. Good luck!"

Sally couldn't help but laugh. Even in her personal life, she was constantly balancing competing needs and adapting to change. It was like running a never-ending Agile project, complete with stakeholder management and shifting requirements.

As she drove home, mentally preparing for the chaos of game night, Sally realized that the principles of Agile – responding to change, focusing on delivering value, and continuously improving – were applicable far beyond the walls of WhisperCorp.

She made a mental note to add another rule to the Sally Model:

> **Rule #10:** *Agile isn't just a work thing. It's a life thing. Embrace change, focus on what matters, and always be ready to adapt... especially when hosting family game night.*

Pulling into her driveway, Sally took a deep breath, steeling herself for the evening ahead. She may not have sticky notes and a whiteboard to help her navigate this particular challenge, but she had something even better – the Agile mindset she'd been cultivating.

As she walked through her front door, greeted by the sound of her family already arguing over which game to play, Sally couldn't help but smile. Life, like Agile, was messy, unpredictable, and full of surprises. But with the right approach, it could also be incredibly rewarding.

"Alright, folks," she announced, channeling her inner Scrum Master, "who's ready for a retrospective on our last game night? I think we have some process improvements to discuss..."

Her family looked at her like she'd grown a second head, but Sally just grinned. The Sally Model was evolving, not just as a framework for work, but as a way of approaching life's challenges with flexibility, humor, and a focus on what really matters.

After their discussion she headed to the kitchen to prepare snacks (vegan options included, of course), Sally couldn't help but feel excited about what the future held, both at WhisperCorp and in her personal life. The Agile journey was far from over, but with each passing day, she was getting better at navigating its twists and turns.

And really, wasn't that what Agile was all about? Continuous improvement, one sticky note at a time.

Manav's Thoughts:

The scene where Sally deciphers conflicting customer feedback instantly takes me back to a workshop I ran. We had sticky notes covering an entire wall—it was like a rainbow exploded! At first, it looked like pure chaos, but that messiness actually led us to some serious clarity. It's such a great example of how Agile doesn't shy away from complexity but instead leans into it to find solutions.

Sally's analogy of balancing customer needs to planning a family reunion dinner? Spot on. I've used similar comparisons in my training sessions, and they always click with people. It's a simple way to show that Agile isn't about making every single person happy—that's impossible. Instead, it's about finding the best path forward when you're juggling a bunch of competing priorities.

The debate between Jenna and Dave about the "auto-generate marketing copy" feature really nails a key Agile principle: figuring out what customers actually need versus what they think they want. It reminded me of Clayton Christensen's "Jobs to be Done" framework. Sometimes the real magic happens when you look past the request and dig into the underlying problem the customer is trying to solve.

Sally's rule about listening to the problem behind the request? Absolute gold. I worked with a team that embraced this idea, and it completely transformed their product. The result? A 200% jump in user engagement. For anyone wanting to dive deeper into this, I always recommend Jeff Patton's *User Story Mapping*. It's a game-changer.

Then there's the team's decision to scrap a feature they spent days building because it became irrelevant. That's Agile in action. It's not easy to let go of something you've put so much effort into, but that willingness to pivot is essential. Eric Ries's *The Lean Startup* dives into this iterative, customer-focused approach and is a must-read for anyone in product development.

When Sally talks about using Agile principles in her personal life, like planning vacations, I couldn't help but nod along. I've encouraged so many clients to try Personal Kanban, and it's amazing how it can boost productivity and create balance. Jim Benson and Tonianne DeMaria Barry really hit the mark with their work on this.

And c Sally's new addition to her model: "Your product is like a garden"? is a perfect way to capture the ongoing care and attention that product development requires. For teams struggling to embrace this mindset, I'd point them toward Ron Jeffries's *The Nature of Software Development*. His organic metaphors for Agile are just brilliant.

Chapter 7

Scaling the Sally Model

Growing Pains and Sticky Note Shortages

Sally McKinnon stood in front of the mirror in her bathroom, practicing her best "I've totally got this under control" face. The results were... less than convincing.

"Come on, Sally," she muttered to her reflection. "You've faced tougher challenges. Remember the Great Caffeine Shortage of 2022? If you can survive that, you can handle scaling the Sally Model."

As she drove to work, Sally couldn't shake the butterflies in her stomach. Word had spread about the success of her custom Agile framework, and now everyone at WhisperCorp wanted a piece of the action. It was like being the only person with snacks at a marathon – suddenly, you're everyone's best friend.

She walked into the office to find a small crowd gathered around her desk. "There she is!" exclaimed Brad from Sales, his voice dripping with enthusiasm. "The Agile Guru herself! When can we get some of that Sally Model magic in our department?"

Sally forced a smile, feeling like a rockstar who'd suddenly been asked to perform brain surgery. "Well, Brad, it's not quite that simple. The Sally Model isn't a one-size-fits-all solution. It needs to be adapted for each team's specific needs."

Brad's face fell faster than a soufflé in an earthquake. "But... but we heard it fixes everything! Can't you just, you know, sprinkle some Agile dust and make the magic happen?"

Sally chuckled, shaking her head. "I'm afraid my supply of Agile dust is running low. But how about we set up a workshop to discuss how we might adapt the model for your team?"

As Brad nodded eagerly and scurried off to spread the news, Sally slumped into her chair. She pulled out her trusty notebook and scribbled a new entry:

Rule #11: *Agile is not magic pixie dust. It's more like sourdough starter – it needs the right environment to thrive, and everyone's batch will be a little different.*

Over the next few weeks, Sally found herself running from one department to another, holding workshops, answering questions, and occasionally putting out fires (both metaphorical and, in one memorable instance involving an overenthusiastic attempt at a "burn-down chart", literal).

In the Marketing department, she walked in on a scene that looked like a paper tornado had hit. Sticky notes covered every available surface, and team members were frantically moving them around.

"Uh, Jenna?" Sally asked, ducking to avoid a flying Post-It. "What's going on here?"

Jenna, her hair wild and eyes slightly manic, turned to Sally. "We're implementing the Sally Model! We're being Agile! Look at all our user stories!"

Sally gently pried a sticky note from Jenna's hand. It read "Make logo more synergistic with cosmic energy." She raised an eyebrow. "Jenna, honey, I think we need to have a chat about what constitutes a user story."

After calming the Marketing team down and explaining that Agile wasn't about generating as many sticky notes as possible, Sally made her way to the Sales department. There, she found a very different scene.

Brad had arranged all the desks in a circle and was leading what appeared to be a cultish chant. "We are Agile! We are flexible! We are the Sally Model incarnate!"

Sally cleared her throat loudly. "Brad? What's happening here?"

Brad beamed at her. "Sally! We're embracing the Agile mindset! We've thrown out all our old processes and we're now completely flexible. No more sales targets, no more customer records – we're just going with the flow!"

Sally pinched the bridge of her nose, feeling a headache coming on. "Brad, being Agile doesn't mean abandoning all structure. It's about finding the right balance between flexibility and stability."

As she spent the next hour explaining to Brad that "embracing change" didn't mean "chaos is king," Sally added another note to her ever-growing list of Sally Model rules:

> **Rule #12:** *Agile is like a good cocktail – it needs the right mix of ingredients, and too much of anything throws off the balance.*

As Sally worked to overcome resistance across different departments, she realized that success hinged on two critical factors: team ownership and stakeholder buy-in.

In the Marketing department, after calming the sticky note chaos, Sally decided to try a different approach.

"Alright, team," she said, "instead of me telling you how to implement the Sally Model, why don't you tell me how you think it could work for Marketing?"

The team exchanged surprised glances. Jenna spoke up hesitantly, "You mean... we get to decide?"

Sally nodded, smiling encouragingly. "Absolutely. You know your work better than anyone. I'm here to guide you, but this needs to be your process."

As the Marketing team began to discuss, their initial resistance transformed into enthusiasm. They weren't being forced to adopt a new methodology; they were creating one that fit their needs.

Meanwhile, in a meeting with top stakeholders, Sally faced a tougher crowd.

"I don't see the point of all this Agile mumbo-jumbo," grumbled one executive. "What's wrong with how we've always done things?"

Sally took a deep breath. "Let me put it this way," she began. "Imagine if we could deliver projects faster, with higher quality, and with the ability to adapt quickly to market changes. That's what we're aiming for with this new approach."

She pulled up a slide showing the improvements they'd already seen in teams that had adopted the Sally Model. As the stakeholders leaned in, their expressions shifting from skepticism to interest, Sally knew she was making headway.

"We're not just changing for the sake of change," she continued. "We're evolving to better meet our business goals and serve our customers. And we need your support to make it happen."

By the end of the meeting, even the most skeptical stakeholders were cautiously on board. Sally left feeling both exhausted and exhilarated. Winning hearts and minds was challenging, but it was the key to making this transformation stick.

As the Sally Model gained traction across different departments, Sally began to see new challenges emerging. Scaling the model across the entire organization wasn't just about replicating what worked in one team—it required a whole new level of coordination and alignment.

"It's like we've mastered making a great cup of coffee," Sally explained to Dave one afternoon, "but now we need to figure out how to run a whole coffee shop chain without losing the quality that made that first cup so good."

Dave nodded thoughtfully. "So, we need to standardize enough to be efficient, but stay flexible enough to meet each department's unique needs?"

"Exactly!" Sally beamed. "And we need to ensure that as we scale, we don't lose sight of our Agile values and principles. It's about creating a shared language and vision across the organization, while still allowing for local adaptation."

She grabbed a marker and started sketching on the whiteboard. "Think of it like a fractal. The core principles remain the same at every level, but the specific implementation might look different depending on where you zoom in."

As Sally and Dave brainstormed ideas for scaling the Sally Model, they realized they were venturing into uncharted territory. But then again, that's what Agile was all about—embracing uncertainty and learning as you go.

By the end of the week, Sally felt like she'd run a marathon while juggling knives. She called an all-hands meeting, determined to address the chaos head-on.

"Alright, everyone," she began, looking out at the sea of eager (and slightly confused) faces. "I know you're all excited about implementing the Sally Model, and that's great. But we need to talk about what that really means."

She drew a large circle on the whiteboard. "Think of the Sally Model like a pizza. The crust is our foundation – our Agile values and principles. That stays consistent. But the toppings?" She started drawing various shapes inside the circle. "Those can vary depending on what each team needs. Some of you might need extra cheese – that's your daily stand-ups. Others might need more pepperoni – that's your sprint planning. The key is finding the right combination that works for your team."

A hand shot up in the back. It was Tom from Product Management. "But Sally, what if we don't like pizza? Can we make it a burrito instead?"

Sally couldn't help but laugh. "Sure, Tom. If a burrito metaphor works better for your team, go for it. The point is, the Sally Model isn't about rigidly following a set of rules. It's about understanding the principles and adapting them to your needs."

As the meeting continued, Sally fielded questions, cleared up misconceptions, and occasionally had to gently remind people that "being Agile" didn't mean they could just do whatever they wanted.

"Remember," she said as the meeting wound down, "the goal of the Sally Model is to help us work more effectively, deliver value to our customers, and hopefully maintain our sanity in the process. It's not about having the most colorful Kanban board or the wackiest stand-up meetings."

As the teams dispersed, chattering excitedly about how they might adapt the Sally Model to their departments, Sally felt a mix of exhaustion and pride. It wasn't going to be an easy journey, but she could see the seeds of real change beginning to take root.

Later that afternoon, as Sally was updating her notes on the Sally Model, Dave from Development approached her desk. "Hey, Sally," he said, looking uncharacteristically sheepish. "I, uh, I think we might have a problem in the Dev team."

Sally braced herself. "What kind of problem, Dave? Did someone try to automate the coffee machine again?"

Dave shook his head. "No, nothing like that. It's just... well, we've been trying to implement the Sally Model, but I think we might be going a bit overboard with the whole 'reflect and adapt' thing."

Sally raised an eyebrow. "How so?"

Dave sighed. "We've been having retrospectives every hour. On the hour. We're spending more time talking about our process than actually, you know, developing anything."

Sally blinked, momentarily at a loss for words. Finally, she managed to say, "Dave, when I said 'at regular intervals,' I didn't mean every sixty minutes."

Dave nodded glumly. "Yeah, I figured we might have misinterpreted that. But you know how developers are – if something's worth doing, it's worth overdoing."

As Sally worked with Dave to find a more reasonable rhythm for the Development team's retrospectives, she couldn't help but reflect on the challenges of scaling the Sally Model. It was like trying to teach a group of cats to line dance – everyone had their own ideas about how it should work, and herding them all in the same direction was a Herculean task.

But as frustrating as it could be, Sally also found it deeply rewarding. With each misunderstanding cleared up, each adaption made, the Sally Model was evolving and improving. It was becoming something greater than she had originally envisioned – a truly flexible framework that could adapt to the needs of diverse teams across WhisperCorp.

As the day drew to a close, Sally added one final note to her list of Sally Model rules:

Rule #13: *Scaling Agile is like raising teenagers—it tests your patience, challenges your authority, and sometimes leaves you pulling your hair out. Yet, with the right guidance, it can also amaze you with its creativity, adaptability, and potential for growth.*

She leaned back in her chair, a satisfied smile playing on her lips. The Sally Model was growing up, finding its place in the wider world of WhisperCorp. It wasn't always pretty, and there were certainly growing pains, but it was happening.

Just then, her phone buzzed with a message from Brad in Sales: "Quick question – for our Agile pizza, can the toppings be sales targets? And if so, how many targets equal one pepperoni?"

Sally chuckled, shaking her head as she typed out a response. The road ahead was long, and undoubtedly filled with more misunderstandings, metaphor mix-ups, and Agile-related mishaps. But as she packed up her things and headed for home, Sally felt a sense of excitement about what the future held.

After all, in the world of Agile – and especially in the world of the Sally Model – every challenge was just another opportunity to inspect, adapt, and improve. And if they could do that while having a few laughs along the way? Well, that was just the cherry on top of their Agile sundae.

Or was it the pepperoni on their Agile pizza?

Sally made a mental note to work on her food-related Agile metaphors. Clearly, that was an area ripe for improvement in the next iteration of the Sally Model.

As she drove home, humming along to the radio, Sally couldn't help but feel a sense of pride in what they'd accomplished. The Sally Model was taking on a life of its own, evolving and adapting in ways she never could have predicted. It was messy, it was challenging, but it was also incredibly exciting.

And really, wasn't that what Agile was all about? Embracing the chaos, learning from the mistakes, and continuously improving. One sticky note, one misunderstood metaphor, one overzealous retrospective at a time.

Sally grinned to herself. Whatever challenges tomorrow might bring, she was ready for them. Armed with her ever-growing list of Sally Model rules, a sense of humor, and an inexhaustible supply of sticky notes, she was prepared to face whatever curveballs the world of Agile – and WhisperCorp – might throw her way.

Let the scaling continue. The Sally Model was just getting started.

Manav's Thoughts:

Sally's struggle with the Finance department's resistance feels all too familiar. Departments like Legal and HR often share the same skepticism, which reminds us that Agile transformations are as much about cultural shifts as they are about new processes. Margaret's comment—"Finance isn't some startup where we can just 'go with the flow'"—hits on a common misunderstanding: Agile is not about chaos but structured flexibility. For those grappling with this, John Kotter's *A Sense of Urgency* offers excellent insights on driving change in established organizations.

Sally's pizza metaphor for explaining the adaptable nature of the Sally Model is brilliant. Analogies like this make complex ideas tangible, and I've used similar ones in workshops. Jonathan Rasmusson's *The Agile Samurai* has some great examples of using metaphors to clarify Agile principles. Meanwhile, the IT team's concerns about "iterating" on server maintenance underscore the need to differentiate between types of work.

Dave's misunderstanding of "regular intervals" for retrospectives—leading to hourly meetings—is both funny and revealing. It highlights the danger of cargo cult Agile, where practices are followed blindly without grasping the underlying principles. Bertrand Meyer's *Agile!: The Good, the Hype and the Ugly* offers a thoughtful critique of these missteps.

The suggestion of an Agile mentorship program is fantastic. Peer learning is incredibly effective in fostering Agile transformations. Esther Derby and Diana Larsen's *Agile Retrospectives: Making Good Teams Great* provides actionable advice on team learning and continuous improvement.

This chapter drives home that scaling Agile is about adaptation, not replication. For organizations embarking on this journey, Craig Larman and Bas Vodde's *Large-Scale Scrum: More with LeSS* is an invaluable resource. Sally's experiences with Marketing and stakeholders underscore two key aspects of Agile transformations: fostering team ownership and securing stakeholder buy-in.

Team ownership means empowering teams to shape their processes, aligning with the Agile principle: "Build projects around motivated individuals. Give them the environment and support they need, and trust them to get the job done." I've seen resistance dissolve when teams move from "implementing Scrum" to discovering their own Agile approach. Engagement skyrockets when people have a say in how they work.

Stakeholder buy-in requires clearly communicating Agile's value in terms that resonate with decision-makers. Translating benefits into business language often helps. For those facing resistance, Chip and Dan Heath's *Switch: How to Change Things When Change Is Hard* offers practical strategies for organizational change. Overcoming resistance isn't about winning arguments; it's about understanding concerns, addressing them collaboratively, and finding common ground. This reflects the Agile value of "Customer collaboration over contract negotiation," with teams and stakeholders as internal customers.

Patience and persistence are key. Transformations take time, but with steady effort and clear communication, even resistant organizations can embrace Agile. Sally's coffee shop analogy perfectly captures the challenge of scaling Agile: maintaining its essence while adapting to the complexities of larger organizations.

Frameworks like SAFe, LeSS, and Nexus offer tools for scaling Agile, but they're not one-size-fits-all. Their principles must be adapted to fit the organization. I recall working with a financial institution that struggled to apply SAFe rigidly. A tailored hybrid approach, blending SAFe and LeSS elements, proved much more effective for their culture and structure.

Ultimately, scaling Agile is about balancing alignment with autonomy and fostering collaboration across the organization. It's not about making everyone work the same way but ensuring teams align on goals while retaining their unique approaches.

Chapter 8

Adapting the Sally Model

When Your Framework Needs a Facelift

Sally McKinnon stood in the conference room, surveying the scene before her with a mix of anticipation and apprehension. It was time for the first company-wide Sally Model retrospective, and the room was buzzing with energy like a beehive.

"Alright, folks," Sally called out, gathering everyone's attention. "Welcome to our grand experiment in continuous improvement. Think of this as a family reunion, but instead of arguing over who makes the best potato salad, we're here to figure out how to make our work lives better."

Dave from Development raised his hand. "Does this mean we can't argue about potato salad? Because I have some strong opinions on that."

Sally chuckled. "Save the potato salad debate for lunch, Dave. For now, let's focus on how the Sally Model has been working for each of your teams."

As the discussion kicked off, Sally couldn't help but marvel at how far they'd come. Just a few months ago, the idea of different departments collaborating like this would have seemed as likely as pigs flying. Now, here they were, sharing experiences and insights across team boundaries.

Jenna from Marketing was the first to speak up. "I have to say, the flexible sprint structure has been a game-changer for us. We can actually adapt to last-minute campaign changes without wanting to tear our hair out... well, most of the time."

Brad from Sales nodded enthusiastically. "And the focus on customer feedback has really helped us tailor our pitches. Although," he added with a grin, "we're still working on translating 'make it pop' into actionable product features."

As the teams shared their experiences, both positive and negative, Sally scribbled notes furiously. It was like watching a complex tapestry being woven before her eyes, each thread representing a different aspect of the Sally Model in action.

But it wasn't all smooth sailing. As the discussion progressed, tensions began to emerge.

Tom from Product Management stood up, his face flushed with frustration. "I'm sorry, but I have to say it. The constant changes are driving us crazy! We can't nail down a product roadmap because everything keeps shifting. How are we supposed to plan for the future?"

Dave jumped in, his voice rising. "That's the point, Tom! We're not supposed to plan everything out in detail. We adapt as we go. You can't predict the future, you can only respond to it!"

Sally could see the situation escalating faster than a rocket launch. She stepped in, her voice calm but firm. "Okay, let's take a breath here. Tom, Dave, you're both making valid points. This is exactly why we're here – to figure out how to balance flexibility with stability."

She turned to the rest of the group. "This is a perfect example of the challenges we face. How can we maintain the agility that Dave's talking about while also providing the stability that Tom needs for effective planning?"

The room fell silent for a moment, everyone pondering the question. Then, to everyone's surprise, it was Brad who spoke up.

"What if," he said slowly, "we treated our product roadmap like a GPS navigation system? We know our ultimate destination, but we're flexible about the route we take to get there. If there's a traffic jam or a closed road, we reroute. But we always know where we're heading."

Sally beamed at Brad, feeling a surge of pride. "That's brilliant, Brad! See, this is exactly the kind of creative problem-solving the Sally Model is all about. We're not just following a set of rules; we're adapting and innovating together."

As the discussion continued, with teams building on Brad's idea and proposing their own solutions, Sally added a new rule to her mental list:

> **Rule #14:** *Feedback isn't just about pointing out problems; it's about collaboratively finding solutions.*

By the end of the session, they had a list of action items longer than the queue at a free coffee stand. But more importantly, there was a palpable sense of energy and ownership in the room. People weren't just passively receiving instructions; they were actively shaping the way they worked.

As the teams filed out, chattering excitedly about the changes they wanted to implement, Sally slumped into a chair, exhausted but exhilarated. She pulled out her notebook, jotting down reflections on the session.

Just then, Dave approached, looking sheepish. "Hey, Sally. I wanted to apologize for getting heated earlier. I guess I got a bit too passionate about the whole 'embrace change' thing."

Sally smiled warmly. "No need to apologize, Dave. Passion is good. We just need to channel it constructively. Besides, if we all agreed all the time, these sessions would be pretty boring, don't you think?"

Dave chuckled. "True. Though I still think we should have that potato salad debate sometime."

As Dave walked away, Sally turned back to her notebook, adding another note:

> **Rule #15:** *Conflict isn't a sign of failure; it's an opportunity for growth. Just like how you need heat to make a good potato salad.*

Later that evening, as Sally was recounting the day's events to her partner over dinner, she had a realization.

"You know," she said, twirling spaghetti around her fork, "this whole continuous feedback thing isn't just for work. We could probably use a bit more of it in our personal lives too."

Her partner raised an eyebrow. "Are you suggesting we start having sprint retrospectives for our relationship?"

Sally laughed. "Well, maybe not quite that formal. But think about it – how often do we really sit down and talk about what's working and what isn't in our lives? Not just the big stuff, but the day-to-day things?"

As they discussed the idea, Sally found herself drawing parallels between her work and personal life. The principles of open communication, continuous improvement, and adapting to change were just as applicable to relationships as they were to software development.

Inspired, Sally proposed a new tradition: a monthly "life retrospective" where they could discuss their goals, challenges, and ways to improve their life together. Her partner agreed, albeit with the caveat that there would be no sticky notes or burndown charts involved.

The next day at work, Sally arrived with a renewed sense of purpose. She gathered the team leads for a quick check-in on how they were implementing the insights from yesterday's retrospective.

"Alright, gang," she said, her energy infectious. "Let's hear how Operation Continuous Improvement is going. Jenna, want to start us off?"

Jenna nodded, her eyes bright with excitement. "We've already made some changes in Marketing. We're trying out a new system for prioritizing campaign tasks, inspired by Brad's GPS metaphor. We call it 'Destination: Customer Delight'."

Brad beamed with pride, while Dave rolled his eyes good-naturedly. "Let me guess," he said, "you've got a slogan and everything?"

Jenna grinned. "You know us too well, Dave. 'Navigate the market, arrive at success!'"

As the other team leads shared their updates, Sally felt a warm glow of satisfaction. The Sally Model was evolving in real-time, shaped by the experiences and insights of the people using it. It wasn't just a framework anymore; it was a living, breathing entity that belonged to all of them.

"Great work, everyone," Sally said as the meeting wrapped up. "Remember, the key to continuous improvement is, well, continuity. Keep the feedback flowing, keep adapting, and don't be afraid to try new things. Even if they don't work out, we'll learn something valuable."

As the team dispersed, Tom lingered behind. "Sally," he said, his voice hesitant, "I've been thinking about what you said yesterday, about balancing flexibility and stability. I think I might have an idea for how we can improve our product roadmap process."

Sally's face lit up. "That's fantastic, Tom! Why don't we grab a coffee and you can tell me all about it?"

As they walked to the cafeteria, Sally marveled at how far they'd come. Just a few months ago, Tom had been one of the most resistant to change. Now, here he was, proposing improvements to the process. It was a powerful reminder of the transformative power of continuous feedback and improvement.

Over the next few weeks, Sally watched with pride as the various teams at WhisperCorp embraced the spirit of continuous feedback. The Sally Model was evolving faster than ever, adapting to the unique needs of each department while maintaining its core principles.

There were still challenges, of course. Change was never easy, and there were days when Sally felt like she was herding cats... very opinionated cats with strong feelings about Agile methodologies. But for every setback, there were moments of breakthrough that made it all worthwhile.

One afternoon, as Sally was updating her ever-growing list of Sally Model rules, she received an email from the CEO. Her heart raced as she opened it, wondering if it was going to be praise or criticism for the recent changes.

To her surprise, it was neither. Instead, it was an invitation to present the Sally Model at an upcoming industry conference. The subject line read: "Time to share our secret sauce with the world?"

Sally leaned back in her chair, a mix of excitement and nervousness washing over her. Sharing the Sally Model with the wider world? That was a big step. But as she thought about how far they'd come, about the enthusiasm and ownership she saw in her colleagues every day, she knew it was the right move.

After all, continuous improvement didn't just apply to their internal processes. It was about continuously pushing their boundaries, taking on new challenges, and yes, sometimes stepping out of their comfort zone.

Sally opened a new document and began to type: "The Sally Model: A Journey of Continuous Adaptation." As she worked on her presentation, she couldn't help but reflect on the parallels between her professional journey and her personal growth.

The principles of the Sally Model – embracing change, focusing on people, and continuous improvement – had seeped into every aspect of her life. From her monthly "life retrospectives" with her partner to the way she approached challenges in her hobbies, Sally realized she had become a living embodiment of the Agile mindset.

As she put the finishing touches on her presentation, Sally added one final rule to her list:

> **Rule #16:** *The journey never ends. There's always room for improvement, always something new to learn. Embrace it, enjoy it, and keep moving forward.*

With a satisfied smile, Sally saved her document and leaned back in her chair. Tomorrow would bring new challenges, new feedback, and new opportunities for growth. But for now, she allowed herself a moment to appreciate how far they'd come.

The Sally Model had started as a simple idea, born out of frustration with rigid processes. Now it was a living, breathing framework that was transforming not just how they worked, but how they thought about work – and life – itself.

As Sally packed up her things to head home, she couldn't help but feel a sense of excitement about what the future held. The Sally Model was ready for its next big adventure, and so was she.

After all, in the world of Agile – and in the world of Sally – the only constant was change. And that was exactly how she liked it.

Manav's Thoughts:

The company-wide Sally Model retrospective scene brought back memories of a large-scale retrospective I once facilitated for a multinational corporation. The energy in the room when diverse teams come together to share experiences is electric. It's a powerful example of how Agile breaks down silos and fosters cross-functional learning.

The tension between Tom from Product Management and Dave from Development over the pace of change reflects a common organizational challenge. It highlights the balance Agile aims for between adaptability and stability. This reminds me of Gartner's "Bi-modal IT" concept, which suggests the need for both stable and agile modes of operation.

Brad's GPS metaphor for the product roadmap is brilliant. I've used similar analogies in consulting, as it captures the essence of Agile planning: having a clear destination but staying flexible about the path. For teams struggling with this, I often recommend Jeff Patton's "User Story Mapping," which provides great techniques for visualizing product development.

Sally applying Agile principles to her personal life, like suggesting a "life retrospective" with her partner, is an idea I've encouraged with clients. Tom's journey from skeptic to contributor is a great example of how Agile transforms mindsets. It's reminiscent of the "Satir Change Model," which outlines the stages people experience when adapting to change. Virginia Satir's work on family systems therapy has many parallels with Agile coaching.

Sally's realization that continuous improvement extends beyond internal processes to how they engage with the world is critical. It connects to Nassim Nicholas Taleb's "Antifragility," the idea that systems can grow stronger through disorder and change.

The addition of "The journey never ends" to the Sally Model rules captures the heart of Agile. It's about continuous improvement, not a fixed destination. This reflects the Japanese concept of "Kaizen," foundational to Lean thinking and Agile.

For anyone wanting to explore the power of continuous feedback and adaptation, I highly recommend "Turn the Ship Around!" by L. David

Marquet. While not specifically about Agile, it offers incredible insights into how continuous learning and empowerment can transform organizations.

Chapter 9

Overcoming Resistance

Converting Skeptics Without Bribery

Sally McKinnon stood outside the door of the Finance department, taking a deep breath as if preparing to enter a lion's den. She'd faced many challenges in her Agile journey at WhisperCorp, but the Finance team's resistance to the Sally Model was proving to be her Everest.

"Alright, Sally," she muttered to herself, "time to channel your inner Agile ninja. Flexibility, empathy, and a dash of humor. You've got this."

As she pushed open the door, she was greeted by a sea of skeptical faces. Leading the pack was Margaret, the head of Finance, whose expression could best be described as "politely murderous."

"Good morning, everyone!" Sally chirped, injecting as much enthusiasm into her voice as she could muster. "I thought we could have a chat about how the Sally Model might work for Finance."

Margaret's eyebrow arched so high it nearly disappeared into her hairline. "Sally, dear," she began, her tone dripping with condescension, "I appreciate your... enthusiasm. But Finance isn't some startup where we can just 'go with the flow.' We deal with hard numbers and strict deadlines. There's no room for your Agile shenanigans here."

Sally felt a flicker of frustration, but she pushed it down. This wasn't the time for defensiveness. Instead, she opted for a different approach.

"You know, Margaret," Sally said, perching on the edge of a nearby desk, "I totally get where you're coming from. When I first heard about Agile, I thought it was some hipster fad, like avocado toast or man buns."

A few chuckles rippled through the room, and Sally saw Margaret's stony expression soften ever so slightly.

"But here's the thing," Sally continued. "Agile, and by extension the Sally Model, isn't about throwing structure out the window. It's about finding a balance between structure and flexibility that allows us to adapt to change more effectively."

Margaret crossed her arms, still looking unconvinced. "And how exactly is that supposed to work in Finance? We can't just change our reporting deadlines on a whim."

Sally nodded, acknowledging the point. "You're absolutely right. And that's why the Sally Model isn't a one-size-fits-all solution. It's more like... a recipe that we can adjust based on each department's needs."

She stood up and walked to the whiteboard, uncapping a marker. "Let's break this down. What are the biggest pain points you face in Finance right now?"

For the next hour, Sally facilitated a lively discussion about the challenges the Finance team faced. As they talked, she jotted down notes on the board, creating a messy but comprehensive map of the department's workflow.

"Okay," Sally said, stepping back to survey their work. "Now, let's look at how some Agile principles might help address these issues."

She circled a note that read "Unexpected last-minute requests from other departments."

"This right here? This is where the flexibility of Agile can be a game-changer. Instead of having a rigid monthly plan, what if we used shorter planning cycles? We could have a 'backlog' of tasks, prioritize the most important ones for each week, and leave some capacity for those unexpected requests."

Margaret frowned, but Sally could see the wheels turning in her head. "But how would we ensure everything gets done?"

Sally grinned. "That's where the 'continuous improvement' part comes in. We'd have regular check-ins – let's call them 'retrospectives' – where we look at what worked, what didn't, and how we can do better next time."

As the discussion continued, Sally could see the resistance starting to crumble. Even Margaret was beginning to engage more positively, asking questions and proposing ideas.

By the end of the session, they had sketched out a rough plan for how the Sally Model could be adapted for Finance. It wasn't perfect, and there were still plenty of details to iron out, but it was a start.

As the team filed out, chattering excitedly about the possibilities, Margaret hung back. "Sally," she said, her voice softer than before, "I have to admit, I may have been too quick to judge. This... Sally Model of yours might have some merit after all."

Sally beamed. "Thanks, Margaret. And thank you for being open to the idea. Remember, the goal here isn't to force you into a box. It's to give you tools to make your work life better."

As Margaret nodded and walked away, Sally added a new rule to her mental list:

> **Rule #17:** *Resistance isn't the enemy; it's an opportunity for deeper understanding and better solutions.*

Over the next few weeks, Sally found herself engaged in similar conversations across WhisperCorp. In the Legal department, she helped the team see how Agile principles could help them manage their heavy caseload more effectively.

"Think of it like a legal buffet," Sally explained to a group of bemused lawyers. "Instead of trying to tackle every case at once, you prioritize, take what you can handle, and come back for more when you're ready."

In IT, she worked with a group of skeptical sys admins who were convinced that Agile was just another management fad.

"Look," said Greg, the head of IT operations, "we can't just 'iterate' on server maintenance. It's not like we can deploy half a security patch and see how it goes."

Sally nodded, understanding his concern. "You're absolutely right, Greg. And that's not what we're suggesting. But what if we applied Agile principles to how we plan and prioritize our IT projects? We could have more frequent check-ins with other departments, adjust our plans based on changing business needs, and maybe even reduce those dreaded midnight emergency calls."

Greg's eyes lit up at that last part. "Reduce midnight calls, you say? Now you're speaking my language."

As Sally worked her way through the company, she found that each conversation, each moment of resistance overcome, added new depth to the Sally Model. It was evolving from a set of rules into a flexible framework that could adapt to the unique needs of each team.

One afternoon, as Sally was updating her notes on the model, Dave from Development stopped by her desk. "Hey, Sally," he said, looking uncharacteristically serious. "Got a minute?"

Sally nodded, gesturing for him to take a seat. "What's up, Dave? Is the Development team having issues with the model?"

Dave shook his head. "No, actually, we're loving it. It's... well, it's the other teams. I've noticed some of them are still struggling, and I thought maybe I could help."

Sally raised an eyebrow, intrigued. "Go on."

"Well," Dave continued, "I remember how skeptical I was at first. But now that I've seen the benefits firsthand, I thought maybe I could talk to some of the other teams. You know, developer to developer, or whatever their equivalent is."

Sally felt a warmth spreading through her chest. This was it – the moment she'd been hoping for. The Sally Model wasn't just her project anymore; it was becoming something the whole company owned and championed.

"Dave," she said, unable to keep the grin off her face, "that's a fantastic idea. In fact, why don't we set up a kind of 'Agile mentorship' program? We could pair up teams that have embraced the model with those still figuring it out."

Dave nodded enthusiastically. "Love it. We could call it the 'Sally Model Buddy System' or something."

As Dave walked away, already making plans for who he could talk to, Sally added another rule:

Rule #18: *True change doesn't come from the top down. It comes when people at all levels embrace and champion the idea.*

The next day, Sally called a company-wide meeting to introduce the new mentorship program. As she looked out at the sea of faces – some excited, some still skeptical, but all engaged – she felt a sense of pride and accomplishment.

"Alright, everyone," she began, "we're entering a new phase of our Agile journey. Up until now, I've been the one pushing the Sally Model. But for it to really work, for it to become part of our company's DNA, it needs to come from all of you."

She explained the mentorship program, emphasizing that it wasn't about forcing the model on anyone, but about sharing experiences and finding ways to make it work for each team.

"Remember," she said, wrapping up her speech, "the Sally Model isn't about following a set of rules. It's about embracing a mindset of continuous improvement, flexibility, and collaboration. It's about making our work lives better, one sticky note at a time."

As the meeting broke up and people began to mingle, discussing potential mentorship pairings, Sally felt a tap on her shoulder. She turned to find the CEO standing there, a broad smile on his face.

"Sally," he said, "I have to hand it to you. When you first proposed this Agile transformation, I thought it was going to be a disaster. But seeing how it's brought the company together, how it's improved our productivity and morale... well, I'm impressed."

Sally felt a blush creeping up her cheeks. "Thank you, sir. But it's not just me. It's everyone here. They're the ones who've really made it work."

The CEO nodded. "And that's the real magic of what you've done. You haven't just implemented a new process. You've created a culture of ownership and improvement."

As the CEO walked away, Sally felt a sense of both accomplishment and anticipation. They'd come so far, but there was still so much potential for growth and improvement.

She pulled out her notebook, flipping to a fresh page. At the top, she wrote: "The Sally Model 2.0 - Embracing Company-Wide Ownership."

As she jotted down ideas, Sally couldn't help but marvel at how far they'd come. From those first chaotic attempts at Agile to this moment of company-wide transformation, it had been quite a journey.

But as any good Agilist knows, the journey is never really over. There would always be new challenges to face, new resistances to overcome, and new opportunities for improvement.

And Sally McKinnon, Agile Coach extraordinaire, creator of the Sally Model, was ready for all of it. Because in the end, that's what Agile – and life – was all about: adapting, learning, and continuously improving.

As she closed her notebook and prepared to dive back into the excited chatter of her colleagues, Sally added one final rule to her list:

Rule #19: *The best frameworks are the ones that eventually make themselves unnecessary. Success is when the Sally Model becomes just 'the way we work'.*

With a satisfied smile, Sally rejoined the group, ready to tackle whatever challenges the next phase of their Agile journey might bring. After all, in the world of Agile, every end was just a new beginning.

And this beginning looked brighter than ever.

Manav's Thoughts:

The scene with Margaret from Finance and her "politely murderous" expression hits close to home. I've seen that same resistance when introducing Agile to traditional, process-heavy departments. It's a stark reminder: Agile transformation isn't just about new processes—it's a cultural shift.

Sally's knack for using humor and relatable analogies to break down resistance is something I've adopted in my own work. Her comparison of Agile to avocado toast and man buns? Hilarious. But it's also effective in making Agile less intimidating. When people see Agile as accessible, they're far more open to trying it.

The Finance team's chaotic first attempt at "being Agile" perfectly illustrates how misunderstandings can derail the process. It reminds me of Ron Jeffries' concept of "Dark Scrum," where poorly applied Agile practices create more problems than they solve. His articles on this topic are essential reading for anyone diving into Agile.

The idea of adapting the "Sally Model" like a recipe is genius. It underscores that Agile isn't one-size-fits-all; it needs to be customized for each team. This mirrors the "Shu Ha Ri" principle from martial arts that I've mentioned previously.

Dave's efforts to help other teams adopt the Sally Model show how Agile fosters shared ownership and continuous improvement. This is reminiscent of the "Spotify Model," where collaboration is strengthened through "Guilds" and "Chapters" to share knowledge across teams.

The CEO's observation about Sally creating a culture of ownership and growth—rather than just implementing a process–aligns with the ideas in Daniel Pink's *Drive* about motivating knowledge workers through autonomy, mastery, and purpose. For anyone facing resistance to Agile adoption, I recommend *Fearless Change: Patterns for Introducing New Ideas* by Mary Lynn Manns and Linda Rising. It's packed with practical strategies for driving organizational change.

Finally, the rule, "The best frameworks are the ones that eventually make themselves unnecessary," is pure gold. It echoes Agile's core principle: "Individuals and interactions over processes and tools." At its heart, Agile is about fostering a mindset and culture—not rigidly following a playbook.

Chapter 10

The Final Reflection

Looking Back Without Falling Over

Sally McKinnon stood at the podium, facing a sea of expectant faces. The annual WhisperCorp company meeting had always been a big deal, but this year felt different. There was an energy in the room, a palpable sense of excitement and accomplishment.

"A year ago," Sally began, her voice steady despite the butterflies in her stomach, "if someone had told me I'd be up here talking about how Agile transformed our company, I'd have laughed. Probably as hard as when Dave tried to automate the coffee machine and turned the break room into a foam party."

A ripple of laughter spread through the audience. Dave, sitting in the front row, gave a mock salute.

"But here we are," Sally continued, a smile playing on her lips. "The Sally Model isn't just a framework anymore—it's part of who we are as a team. And let me tell you, getting here was about as smooth as a rollercoaster in an earthquake."

As Sally launched into her speech, recounting the ups and downs of their Agile journey, her mind wandered back to where it all began. She remembered the chaos of those first few months, the resistance, the confusion, the late nights fueled by nothing but coffee and sheer determination.

There was the time Brad from Sales tried to turn their Kanban board into a dartboard, claiming it would "add an element of excitement to task allocation." Or the day the Finance team, in a misguided attempt to be more Agile, decided to do their quarterly report as an interpretive dance. Margaret's portrayal of the Q3 earnings as a series of increasingly frantic pirouettes was something Sally would never forget, no matter how hard she tried.

But for every misstep, there were moments of brilliance. When the Development team, inspired by the principle of continuous improvement, created a bot that automatically ordered pizza whenever a project was successfully completed. (They had to tweak that one after Dave gained ten pounds in a month, but the spirit was there.)

Or the time the Marketing team used Agile principles to pivot a failing campaign mid-flight, turning a potential disaster into their most successful promotion ever. Jenna still swore that the "Embrace the Chaos" slogan was divinely inspired during a particularly intense sprint planning session.

As Sally spoke, she could see the transformation reflected in the faces of her colleagues. Gone was the skepticism, the resistance, the fear of change. In its place was confidence, enthusiasm, and a shared sense of purpose.

Sally's expression softened as she shifted gears. "But the Sally Model isn't just about work processes. It's about how we approach challenges everywhere—in our lives, our relationships, our goals."

She paused, taking a sip of water, before diving into a more personal reflection.

She paused, leaning slightly toward the audience. "Want to know a secret? I started applying Agile at home. Turns out, sprint planning doesn't go so well when your stakeholder is a cat who thinks knocking things off shelves is a feature, not a bug."

Laughter rippled through the room.

"But jokes aside, embracing an Agile mindset has truly transformed how I approach life's challenges. I've learned to be more flexible, to embrace change rather than fear it. I've discovered the power of breaking big, scary goals into smaller, manageable tasks. And most importantly, I've learned the value of continuous reflection and improvement."

Sally's voice took on a more serious tone. "I used to think that being successful meant having everything figured out, having a perfect plan and sticking to it no matter what. But Agile has taught me that true success comes from being adaptable, from being willing to learn and grow and change course when necessary."

She looked out at the audience, making eye contact with familiar faces. Dave, who had gone from skeptic to champion. Margaret, who had discovered a hidden talent for creative problem-solving. Brad, who had finally learned that "make it pop" was not a valid user story.

"Each of you," Sally said, her voice filled with warmth, "has been an integral part of this journey. You've taken the Sally Model and made it your own. You've adapted it, improved it, and in doing so, you've made our company stronger and more resilient than ever before."

As Sally wrapped up her speech, she felt a sense of closure, but also of new beginnings. The Sally Model had evolved far beyond her initial vision, shaped by the collective experiences and insights of everyone at WhisperCorp.

As she wrapped up, Sally smiled. "So what's next for us? Well, if Agile's taught us anything, it's that the journey never ends. There will always be new challenges, new opportunities. But now, we face them together—with a mindset of adaptation and growth."

As the applause washed over her, Sally felt a mixture of pride, gratitude, and excitement for what the future held. She stepped down from the podium, immediately surrounded by well-wishers and colleagues eager to share their own Agile success stories.

Later that evening, as Sally sat in her living room, reflecting on the day's events, she couldn't help but marvel at how far they'd come. She pulled out her trusty notebook, flipping through pages filled with rules, observations, and the occasional coffee stain.

"The Sally Model," she murmured, tracing the words on the first page. It had started as a desperate attempt to bring order to chaos, and had grown into something so much more.

Just then, her phone buzzed with a message. It was from Dave: "Great speech today, boss. Quick question - do you think we could apply Agile principles to planning the company picnic? I have some ideas involving user stories for potato salad..."

Sally chuckled, shaking her head as she typed out a response. Some things never changed. And yet, everything had changed.

As she settled in for the evening, Sally's mind wandered to the future. What new challenges would they face? How would the Sally Model continue to evolve? She didn't have all the answers, but for the first time in her career, that didn't scare her. If anything, it excited her.

Because that was the beauty of Agile, wasn't it? It wasn't about having all the answers. It was about being ready and willing to find them, together.

Sally picked up a pen and opened her notebook to a fresh page. At the top, she wrote: "The Sally Model: The Next Chapter."

As she began to jot down ideas, a smile played on her lips. The journey wasn't over. In many ways, it was just beginning. And Sally McKinnon, Agile champion extraordinaire, was ready for whatever came next.

After all, in the world of Agile, every ending was just a new beginning in disguise. And this beginning? It looked brighter than ever.

Sally closed her notebook, feeling a sense of contentment wash over her. She had started this journey hoping to bring order to chaos, to find a better way of working. What she had found was so much more – a new way of thinking, a new way of approaching life itself.

The Sally Model wasn't just a framework anymore. It was a testament to the power of adaptability, of collaboration, of continuous improvement. It was proof that with the right mindset, any challenge could be overcome, any goal could be achieved.

As she drifted off to sleep that night, Sally's dreams were filled not with Kanban boards or sprint backlogs, but with endless possibilities. In her mind's eye, she saw a future where the principles of Agile weren't just confined to the workplace but were embraced in all aspects of life. A future where people approached challenges with flexibility and creativity, where continuous improvement was the norm rather than the exception.

And in that future, Sally saw herself not as the creator of the Sally Model, but as a fellow traveler on this never-ending journey of growth and adaptation. Because in the end, that's what Agile was all about – not a destination, but a way of moving through the world.

As the first rays of sunlight peeked through her curtains, Sally awoke with a smile on her face and a spring in her step. Another day, another opportunity to learn, to grow, to improve.

She grabbed her notebook, flipped to a new page, and wrote:

> **Rule #20:** *The best framework is the one that teaches you to think beyond frameworks. Embrace the Agile mindset, and the rest will follow.*

With that, Sally McKinnon, Agile enthusiast and accidental revolutionary, set off to face another day. The Sally Model might have reached its final form, but the journey? The journey was just getting started.

And Sally couldn't wait to see where it would take them next.

Manav's Thoughts:

The scene of Sally addressing the annual company meeting is a powerful culmination of the Agile journey. It reminds me of the transformations I've witnessed in organizations where Agile becomes more than just a methodology - it becomes a part of the company's DNA.

Sally's reflection on the early chaos, like Brad's dartboard Kanban and Finance's interpretive dance report, humorously highlights a crucial point: the path to true Agile adoption is often messy and filled with misunderstandings. Like Tuckman's stages of group development: forming, storming, norming, and performing. Many teams get stuck in the storming phase, but pushing through leads to real breakthroughs.

The Development team's pizza-ordering bot is a fantastic example of how Agile principles can spark innovation in unexpected ways. It reminds me of Google's famous 20% time policy, which allowed employees to work on side projects, leading to innovations like Gmail and Google News.

Sally's application of Agile principles to her personal life, like sprint planning for household chores, is something I always encourage. It's a testament to how Agile can become a mindset that permeates all aspects of life.

The evolution of the Sally Model from a desperate attempt to bring order to chaos into a company-wide philosophy of continuous improvement is beautiful. It echoes the journey many organizations go through, from "doing Agile" to "being Agile".

Sally's final reflection on Agile being about adaptability, collaboration, and continuous improvement rather than just following frameworks is the "Heart of Agile" concept developed by one of the original Agile Manifesto signatories, Alistair Cockburn, which distills Agile down to four key principles: Collaborate, Deliver, Reflect, and Improve.

Epilogue

The Ripple Effect

Five years after the full adoption of the Sally Model at WhisperCorp, Sally McKinnon found herself standing on a stage at an international Agile conference, preparing to give the keynote address. As she looked out at the sea of faces, she marveled at how far the ripples of their little experiment had spread.

"When we started our Agile journey," Sally began, her voice calm and confident, "we thought we were just trying to improve our work processes. What we didn't realize was that we were embarking on a shift in how we approach problems, collaborate, and create value."

She paused, letting her words sink in.

"Today, I want to talk about some of the less obvious, but equally important, aspects of Agile that we discovered along the way. Things that didn't make it into the official Sally Model documentation, but became integral to our success."

Sally clicked to her first slide, which simply read: "Courage."

"Agile requires courage," she continued. "Courage to admit when we're wrong, courage to try new things, courage to be transparent about our progress and our setbacks. At WhisperCorp, we learned that fostering a culture of psychological safety was crucial to building this courage."

She shared an anecdote about how the Development team had instituted a "Failure of the Week" award, celebrating the team member who had taken the biggest risk or learned the most valuable lesson from a mistake. What started as a joke became a powerful tool for encouraging innovation and resilience.

The next slide read: "Respect."

"Respect is at the core of every successful Agile team," Sally explained. "It's not just about being polite. It's about truly valuing each team member's contributions, background, and unique perspective."

She talked about how WhisperCorp had implemented cross-functional "shadowing" days, where team members would spend a day learning about each other's roles. This not only improved collaboration but also deepened mutual respect and understanding across the organization.

As Sally moved through her presentation, she touched on other crucial aspects of Agile that often go unmentioned:

1. **Sustainable Pace:** We learned the hard way that constant sprinting leads to burnout. We had to find a rhythm that allowed for both high productivity and long-term sustainability.
2. **Technical Excellence:** Agile isn't just about moving fast; it's about building things right. We invested heavily in continuous learning and improving our technical practices.
3. **Simplicity:** We often find ourselves asking, 'What's the simplest thing that could possibly work?' This mindset helped us avoid over-engineering and focus on delivering real value.
4. **Customer Collaboration:** We moved beyond just gathering requirements to truly partnering with our customers throughout the development process.
5. **Responding to Change:** We learned to see change not as a disruption, but as an opportunity to create something even better than we had originally planned.

As Sally neared the end of her talk, she pulled up a final slide. It was a photo of the WhisperCorp team at their last company picnic, all wearing t-shirts that read "Agile is a Mindset, Not a Rulebook."

"This," Sally said, her voice filled with pride, "is the real success of our Agile transformation. Not the improved metrics, not the faster delivery times, though those are certainly nice. The real success is that we've created a culture where adaptability, continuous improvement, and collaboration are just how we do things."

She paused, looking out at the audience. "Agile isn't a set of practices you follow. It's a way of thinking, a way of approaching challenges. It's about valuing individuals and interactions, embracing change, and constantly striving to be better than you were yesterday."

As Sally wrapped up her speech, she felt a sense of completion. The Sally Model had evolved beyond her wildest dreams, touching not just processes, but people's lives and mindsets.

"So, my fellow Agilists," she concluded, "I challenge you to look beyond the frameworks and methodologies. Embrace the Agile mindset in all aspects of your life. Be courageous, be respectful, be collaborative. Seek simplicity, strive for excellence, and always, always be ready to learn and adapt."

The applause was thunderous as Sally stepped away from the podium. As she made her way off the stage, she couldn't help but smile. The journey that had started with a frustrated business analyst trying to bring order to chaos had turned into a movement that was changing the way people worked and lived.

And the best part? It was still evolving, still adapting, still improving. Because that's what Agile was all about. It wasn't a destination to be reached, but a never-ending journey of growth and discovery.

As Sally joined the crowd, ready to learn and share and grow even more, she knew that the next chapter of the Agile story was yet to come. And she couldn't wait to see where it would lead.

Manav's Thoughts:

First of all, congratulations on making it to the end of Sally's Agile journey! You've just completed a significant step toward mastering the fundamentals of Agile and, more importantly, embracing a mindset of continuous improvement. But as we know, the real beauty of Agile lies in its ability to grow with us. Just as Sally and her team evolved, your Agile journey is just beginning.

The scene of Sally giving a keynote at an international Agile conference five years later is a powerful image. It represents not just personal growth, but the ripple effect that one team's Agile journey can have on the wider community. This reminds me of the concept of "positive deviance" in change management - how localized success can drive wider transformation.

Sally's focus on the less obvious aspects of Agile is a representation of how teams focus on the practices and lose sight of the underlying principles and values. The emphasis on courage, respect, and psychological safety echoes the work of Amy Edmondson on teaming and psychological safety in the workplace.

The "Failure of the Week" award is a brilliant way to encourage risk-taking and learning, reminds me of how Pixar uses the concept of "plussing" - building on ideas without using judgmental language - to create a culture of creativity and continuous improvement.

The discussion on sustainable pace is vital. Many organizations miss this crucial aspect of Agile, leading to burnout and reduced quality. The book "Slack: Getting Past Burnout, Busywork, and the Myth of Total Efficiency" by Tom DeMarco offers great insights into the importance of building slack into systems.

The emphasis on technical excellence is often overlooked in Agile transformations. Robert Martin's concept of "Clean Code" and the broader software craftsmanship movement offer valuable perspectives on maintaining technical quality in an Agile environment.

The focus on simplicity - "What's the simplest thing that could possibly work?" - is a powerful Agile principle. It reminds me of the

YAGNI (You Ain't Gonna Need It) principle in software development, which helps teams avoid over-engineering and focus on delivering value.

Dear readers, thank you for embarking on this Agile journey with Sally and the WhisperCorp team. Remember, this is just the beginning. Agile is not a destination, but a continuous journey of learning and improvement. I encourage you to stay curious, to experiment, and to always seek a deeper understanding of Agile principles.

If you've discovered interesting concepts or have experiences that you think could enhance the Sally Model, I'd love to hear from you. Your insights could be invaluable in shaping future versions of this story, and of course, you'd be fully acknowledged for your contributions.

This journey doesn't end here. Agile is a vast field with many interconnected concepts and methodologies. If you're interested in exploring more topics - perhaps diving deeper into specific Agile frameworks, exploring the intersection of Agile with other disciplines, or even looking at how Agile principles can be applied in non-software contexts - please reach out. Your interest and feedback will guide the development of future series.

Remember, the heart of Agile is about continuous improvement, both in our work and in ourselves. As you go forward, keep questioning, keep learning, and keep adapting. The Agile mindset is a powerful tool not just for work, but for life.

Thank you for joining me on this journey. Here's to many more adventures in the world of Agile!

ABOUT THE AUTHOR

Manav Agarwal is an experienced Agile Transformation Leader and Coach with a passion for promoting agile mindsets in organizations. With a career spanning over a decade in the tech industry, Manav has established himself as a driving force in the agile community and is known for his innovative approaches to implementing Scrum and SAFe® in various environments.

With an engineer's mind and a teacher's heart, Manav's journey into the world of Agile began during his academic days at the prestigious IIT Bombay. There, he honed his skills in aerospace engineering while discovering his talent for breaking down complex concepts into easily understandable parts.

His thinking has been shaped by international experience, including a Masters in Project Management in France and studies at the University of Toronto in Canada. This multicultural background enables him to adapt agile principles to different cultural contexts, making him a versatile coach in the global business world.

His professional journey has taken him through renowned companies such as Airbus, Hager, and Alten, where he has always proven his ability to lead teams, implement agile methods, and drive digital transformations. But it was at Siemens where Manav found his true calling as an Agile Transformation Leader.

As a SAFe® Program Consultant (SPC) and PMI Agile Certified Practitioner (PMI-ACP®), Manav has trained and coached hundreds of professionals in agile methods and SAFe. His workshops are known for their hands-on and interactive approach, enriched with real-world anecdotes and a touch of humor - a skill he has perfected through his hobby of stand-up comedy.

In his role as an adult education trainer, Manav regularly conducts workshops on the agile mindset, reaching a wider audience by spreading the agile philosophy beyond the tech industry. His ability to combine technical expertise with soft skills makes his trainings both informative and transformative.

Manav's approach to agile coaching is holistic and people-centered. He believes that true agility goes beyond processes and tools - it's about fostering a mindset of continuous improvement, adaptability, and collaboration. His experience in various industries - from aerospace to renewable energy - has given him unique insights into the application of agile principles in different contexts.

With his combination of technical expertise, teaching talent, and infectious enthusiasm for all things agile, Manav continues to inspire and guide individuals and organizations on their agile transformation journey. His ultimate goal? To spread the agile mindset not only in IT teams but throughout organizations and beyond to create a more adaptive, collaborative, and innovative world.

www.ingramcontent.com/pod-product-compliance
Lightning Source LLC
Chambersburg PA
CBHW070352230526
45471CB00006B/2525